DOLCI & FRUTTA

Cakes & Desserts the Italian Way

Text by Rosalba Gioffrè
Photography by Marco Lanza
Set Design by Rosalba Gioffrè

MᶜRAE BOOKS

Other titles in the same series:
Pastissima! Pasta the Italian Way
Antipasti! Appetizers the Italian Way
Verdure! Vegetables the Italian Way
Zuppe Risotti Polenta! Italian Soup, Rice & Polenta Dishes
Pizza Pane Focacce! Pizza, Bread & Focacce the Italian Way
Pesce! Fish & Seafood the Italian Way
Carne! Meat Dishes the Italian Way

Conceived, edited, and designed by McRae Books
Publishers: Anne McRae, Marco Nardi

Text: Rosalba Gioffrè
Photography: Marco Lanza
Set Design: Rosalba Gioffrè
Design: Marco Nardi

Translation from the Italian: Sara King
Editing: Alison Leach and Anne McRae
Color separations: Fotolito Toscana, Florence, Italy

The publishers would like to thank Mastrociliegia (Fiesole), Pasquinucci
(Florence) and Mrs. Ines for their assistance during the production of this book.

ISBN 88-88166-36-x

Printed and bound in Italy by Artegrafica, Verona

CONTENTS

INTRODUCTION

The recipes in this book are all modern interpretations of traditional Italian cakes, desserts, and cookies that can be made with ease at home, even by novice cooks. We begin with a baking basics section featuring ingredients and eleven classic recipes, including short crust and puff pastry, vanilla pastry cream (and variations), zabaione, meringues, Italian sponge cake, sugar syrup, and crêpes. These recipes are referred to throughout the book, so it might be worthwhile having a look at them first. The main part of the book is divided into five chapters, starting with cakes and pies. This is the largest section and it contains a wonderful array of recipes, especially for pies and tarts, which are staples for the Italian pastry cook. Subsequent chapters are on scrumptious creamy desserts, wholesome cookies, wicked fritters and crêpes, and healthy fruit and ice-cream. Italian cuisine is justifiably famous for its pasta, pizza, and appetizers, but it is also capable of dazzling in the sweeter realms of confectionary. Discover the lesser known pleasures of Italian Dolci. Serve them to your family and friends, and... Enjoy!

BASIC INGREDIENTS

Basic baking ingredients include flour, sugar, milk, butter, and egg—staples in any kitchen. However, there are many different types of flour, for example, and learning to distinguish them and their various uses, will help you create the perfect cake or dessert every time. The ingredients on these pages will almost all be very familiar to you. Before attempting any of the recipes in this book, make sure you have all the ingredients and that they are of good quality and very fresh.

CORNMEAL
Fine or coarsely ground, cornmeal is used in many regional recipes.

RYE FLOUR
For best results, rye flour should be mixed with white flour.

SOFT WHEAT FLOUR
In Italy, the soft wheat flour used for baking comes in two types, labeled "00" and "0." The first is highly refined and is used for delicate recipes, such as cakes and desserts. The second, type "0" flour is slightly less refined. The recipes in this book will all work with high quality all-purpose (plain) or cake flours.

LEAVENING AGENTS
Most of the cakes, cookies, and desserts in this book are leavened using baking powder, which is a mixture of acid-reacting salts and sodium bicarbonate. Some also make use of baking soda, or active dry or fresh yeast (shown left).

EGGS
The eggs in the recipes in this book have all been calculated as weighing in at about 2 oz (60 g). For best results when baking, always use eggs at room temperature rather than straight from the refrigerator.

LARD
Lard is obtained by mixing different types of pork fat together. In traditional Italian cooking, it is used to fry some sweets and also in some doughs.

SUGAR

Most cakes and desserts call for superfine granulated (caster) sugar, which dissolves more easily.

DEMERARA SUGAR

Less refined than white sugar. Can be substituted with ordinary brown sugar in most recipes.

CONFECTIONERS' SUGAR

Also known as icing sugar, it should always be sifted before use.

CREAM

Cow's cream can be used fresh as is, or beaten until thick. Cooking cream is also available.

MASCARPONE CHEESE

This very rich cheese is made from cow's cream. It is used in many desserts, including cheesecakes and Tiramisù.

BUTTER

Remember that most Italian butter is unsalted, so be careful when adding extra salt to a cake or cookie recipe.

YOGURT

Yogurt is a recent addition to the Italian baking repertoire. It is mainly served fresh with fruit dishes.

RICOTTA CHEESE

Ricotta is a fresh cheese made from ewe's or cow's milk. Mixed with eggs, sugar, and vanilla, it is used to make mousses and other creamy desserts.

MILK

The recipes in this book all make use of pasteurized cow's milk.

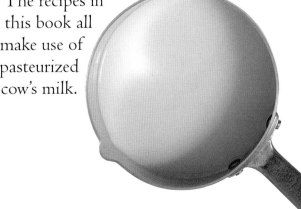

SPICES, FLAVORINGS, AND OTHER INGREDIENTS

The taste, consistency, and appearance of many cakes, cookies, and desserts depend on the spices, nuts, and food colorings or flavorings they contain. Most Italian recipes do not make use of hard-to-find or expensive ingredients.

CRACKED WHEAT
This is the main ingredient in the traditional Neapolitan Ricotta pie (see recipe, page 48).

CHOCOLATE
All high-quality dark chocolates can be used in baking, although bittersweet and semi-sweet usually have a stronger chocolate flavor.

RICE
The rice grown in Italy is all short-grain. The small, plump "Originario" is usually the best for Italian recipes.

PEARL BARLEY
A grain from which the tough outer hull has been removed.

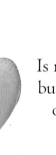

WHITE CHOCOLATE
Is made with cocoa butter, sugar, milk, and other flavorings.

HONEY
Many old-fashioned or regional recipes include honey.

CANDIED FRUIT

COFFEE
Is often used to flavor creams, frostings, icings, and ice-cream.

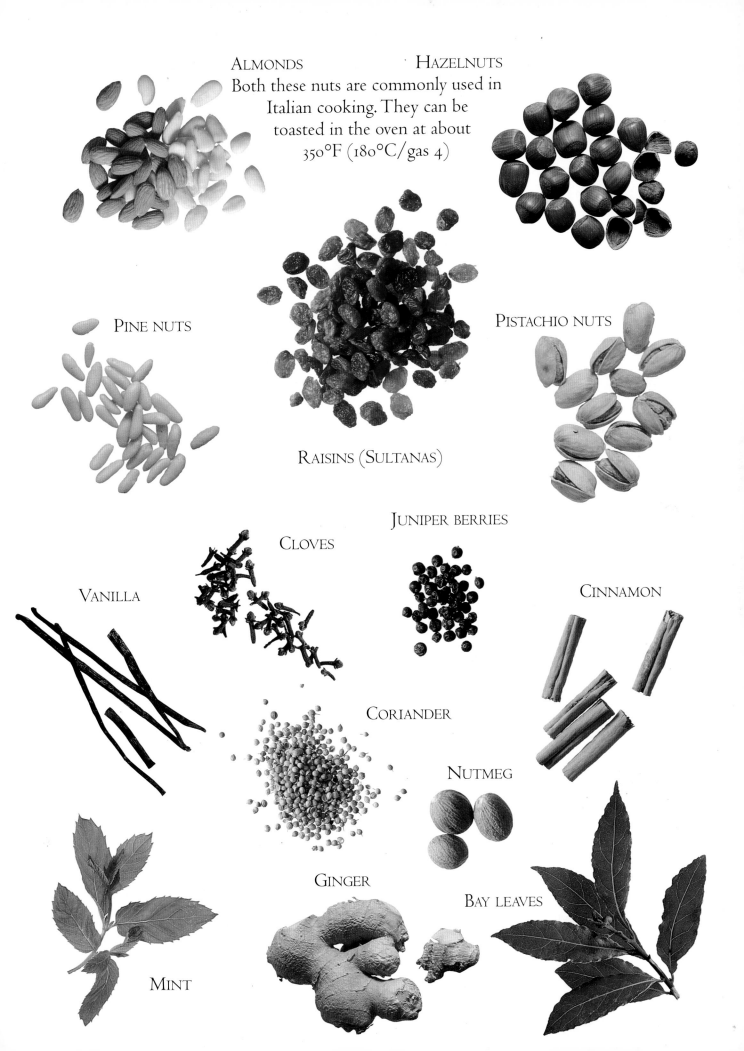

ALMONDS   HAZELNUTS
Both these nuts are commonly used in
Italian cooking. They can be
toasted in the oven at about
350°F (180°C/gas 4)

PINE NUTS   PISTACHIO NUTS

RAISINS (SULTANAS)

JUNIPER BERRIES

CLOVES

VANILLA   CINNAMON

CORIANDER

NUTMEG

GINGER

BAY LEAVES

MINT

PASTA FROLLA
Sweet plain pastry

This crumbly, melt-in-the-mouth pastry is used as a base for many pies. It is easy to make, but there are one or two things to bear in mind. Firstly, although the dough must be well-mixed, it should not be kneaded for too long or it will become tough. Work quickly when kneading. You may prefer to divide the mixture in half and knead separately. Remember, too, that this pastry improves with time, so it is best made a day ahead.

Makes: pastry to line and cover a 10-in (25-cm) pan; Preparation: 10 minutes + 30 minutes to chill; Cooking: 30 minutes; Level of difficulty: Simple

Combine the flour with the sugar and salt and add the lemon zest, if using. § Transfer to a floured work surface and shape into a mound. Make a well in the center and drop the butter into it. § Knead the mixture as quickly as possible with your fingertips to obtain a dough resembling fine bread crumbs. § Shape the mixture into a mound, make a well in the center and drop the egg yolks into it. Knead until smooth, then shape into a ball. Wrap the dough with plastic wrap and chill in the refrigerator for at least 30 minutes. § Roll out the dough and place in a buttered and floured springform pan. Prick the base all over with a fork to prevent air bubbles forming. § At this point, depending on the recipe, the dough can either be covered with a filling and cooked or baked "blind." If baking blind, cover the dough with a sheet of baking paper and sprinkle with dry beans or peas to stop the pastry from rising during cooking. Bake in a preheated oven at 350°F/180°C/gas 4 for about 30 minutes.

INGREDIENTS

- 2½ cups (8 oz/250 g) all-purpose (plain) flour
- ⅓ cup (3 oz/90 g) sugar
- dash of salt
- dash of grated lemon zest, yellow part only (optional)
- ½ cup (4 oz/125 g) butter, chopped into small pieces
- 2 egg yolks

PASTA BRISÉ
Short crust pastry

This pastry is similar to the one above, except that it contains no egg. Mainly used without sugar for savories, it is sometimes used for pies and tarts.

Makes: enough pastry to line and cover a 10-in (25-cm) pan; Preparation: 20 minutes + 30 minutes to chill; Cooking: 20 minutes; Level of difficulty: Simple

Pour the sifted flour, salt, and sugar onto a clean work surface. Make a well in center of the flour and fill with the butter. Work the mixture with rapid movements of the balls of the thumbs until it is the consistency of coarse sand. § Shape this mixture into a mound, make a well in the center, and fill with the water. Work the water into the butter and flour. Shape the dough into a ball, wrap in plastic wrap, and chill in the refrigerator. Use as directed in the recipes, or freeze for later use.

INGREDIENTS

- 2½ cups (8 oz/250 g) all-purpose (plain) flour
- dash of salt
- 1 tablespoon sugar (optional)
- ½ cup (4 oz/125 g) butter, cut in small pieces
- about ½ cup (4 fl oz/ 125 ml) warm water

Right:

Pasta frolla

Pasta sfoglia
Puff pastry

*Puff pastry is the most versatile and delicious of all the various pastry doughs.
It is made using the same basic ingredients — flour, water, butter, and salt — but
the dough is much richer, and more intriguing. It garners its special qualities during
the repeated rolling and folding process involved in its making. The butter,
which is added as a single layer, is folded and rolled within the pastry,
creating layer on layer of paperthin sheets of dough separated by equally
thin layers of butter. During baking the butter melts, releasing steam that
causes the dough to rise and puff. Remember that puff pastry's reputation
for being complicated, time-consuming, and temperamental has been
exaggerated and that with a little time and practice, most cooks can
master its secrets.*

- 2 cups (7 oz/200 g)
  all-purpose (plain) flour
- dash of salt
- dash of sugar
- about 1 cup (8 fl oz/
  250 ml) water
- 1 cup (8 oz/250 g) butter,
  softened

Serves: 4-6; Preparation: 50 minutes + 30 minutes to rest; Level of difficulty: Complicated

Sift the flour and salt in a mound on a clean work surface and make a
well in the center. Dissolve the sugar in the water and pour about half
the water into the well in the flour. Using your hands, mix the
ingredients until the dough is about the same consistency as the
softened butter. Adjust the dough to achieve the required consistency
by adding flour or water. § Roll the dough into a ball, wrap in plastic
wrap and set aside for 30 minutes. § Use a rolling pin to roll the
dough out on a floured work surface into a square shape about ½ in
(1 cm) thick. § Cut the softened butter in pieces and place them at
the center of the square. Fold the 4 sides of the square so that the
butter is completely sealed in, and roll the dough out in a rectangular
shape about ½ in (1 cm) thick. § Fold the rectangle in 3, turn the
folded dough, and roll it out again. Fold it again and let stand for
about 10 minutes. § Repeat this operation 3 times, letting the dough
rest each time for 10 minutes. § Roll out to ¼ in (1 cm) thickness and
use as indicated in the recipes.

VARIATION
– Use half all-purpose (plain) flour and half unbleached white
pastry flour for a stronger dough that can be rolled without
breaking or tearing.

Right:
Pasta sfoglia

CRESPELLE

Crêpes

Crêpes are small pancakes made with milk, egg, and flour. They are never eaten on their own but are used as the basis for countless sweet and savory recipes.

Makes: 10-12 crêpes; Preparation: 10 minutes + 2 hours to rest; Cooking: 30 minutes; Level of difficulty: Simple

Beat the eggs, sugar, and salt with the sifted flour. § Pour in the milk gradually, followed by the melted butter. Beat the batter until smooth then set aside to rest for 2 hours. § Brush a small, heated skillet (frying pan) with the remaining butter, and add a small ladleful of batter. Spread evenly by tipping the pan, so that it forms a thin film. Cook the crêpe on both sides, taking care not to let it color too much. When the edges curl slightly, it is done. § If not using immediately, crêpes can be stored in the refrigerator, piled one on top of the other in a covered container.

VARIATIONS
– Flavor the batter with two tablespoonfuls of rum or cognac.
– Other types of flour can also be used in the making of crêpes, such as buckwheat or whole-meal.

■ INGREDIENTS

- 2 eggs
- 1 teaspoon sugar
- dash of salt
- 1 cup (4 oz/125 g) all-purpose (plain) flour
- 1 cup (8 fl oz/250 ml) milk
- 1½ tablespoons butter, melted, plus 1 teaspoon butter, at room temperature, to grease the pan

PAN DI SPAGNA

Italian sponge cake

This recipe dates back to the 17th century. As the Italian name implies, this sponge cake was introduced to Italy by the Spaniards. In addition to its use in layer cakes and puddings, it can also be sliced and toasted for breakfast.

Serves: 6; Preparation: 30 minutes; Cooking: 40 minutes; Level of difficulty: Medium

Place the eggs and sugar in the top part of a double boiler and whisk until frothy. § Remove from heat and add the lemon zest (yellow part only) and continue to whisk until cool. § Fold in the sifted flours and salt gently, using slow movements and keeping the blade of the spatula pointing downward. Pour the dough into a greased, floured 10-in (25-cm) springform pan and bake in a preheated oven at 325°F/160°C/gas 3 oven for 40 minutes.

VARIATIONS
– Whisk the eggs in the top half of a double-boiler. The heat will make them coagulate slightly, providing a better base for the flour and making it easier for the dough to rise.
– Sponge cake can be flavored to taste with vanilla extract (essence).

■ INGREDIENTS

- 6 eggs
- ¾ cup (5 oz/150 g) sugar
- 2 teaspoons grated lemon zest
- ¾ cup (3 oz/90 g) all-purpose (plain) flour
- dash of salt
- ¾ cup (3 oz/90 g) potato flour (potato starch)

Right:
Pan di Spagna

Panna montata
Whipped cream

Whipped cream is easy to prepare. It is widely used in confectionery for cake decoration, filling for meringues and small items of confectionery, and as a garnish for fruit-based preparations. It is also an ingredient in complicated jellycreams, or quite simply used to top a cup of hot chocolate.

Serves: 6; Preparation: 5–10 minutes; Level of difficulty: Simple

Place the cream in a mixing bowl. Both the cream and the bowl should be well-chilled. Use a large bowl, since cream doubles in bulk as it fills with air. § If using an electric whisk, add the sugar first, and begin beating slowly at first, increasing the speed after a few minutes, until the cream is stiff. If using a hand-whisk, carefully add the sugar toward the end. § Do not overbeat because the cream will turn into butter. Whipped cream should always be used immediately, as it tends to collapse and separate very quickly.

Caramello
Sugar syrup

Sugar syrup is not difficult to make, although it does require extreme care. To prepare the syrup, you will need a heavy-bottomed saucepan, preferably one made of thick-gauge copper, as this ensures even cooking. Do not use a tin-plated saucepan; sugar melts at a very high temperature and may cause the tin to melt. Professional confectioners measure the degree to which sugar is cooked by using a Baumé scale or a candy thermometer. We have suggested a series of "stages," to be used in home cooking.

Put three parts sugar and one of water in a heavy-bottomed pan and add a few drops of lemon juice to prevent crystallization. Place the saucepan over medium heat, and when the liquid starts to boil, use a moistened pastry brush to remove the froth that will form at the sides. Never stir the liquid, as the cold spoon would cause the sugar to crystallize. § As soon as a thick layer of bubbles starts to form, the sugar will pass through the following stages, from which it is possible to tell how far it is cooked: GLAZING: this is the initial stage. At this point, if you dip a spatula into the liquid it will be coated with a thin film of syrup. THIN THREAD: if you take a little sugar between two fingers it forms a fine thread that breaks easily. STRONG THREAD: as above but the thread is stronger. FEATHERY: if you remove a little of the sugar from the pan with a perforated spoon and blow through it, bubbles form. SOFT BALL: if you dip a little of the sugar in cold water and hold it between two fingers it forms a soft elastic ball. FIRM BALL: a firmer ball forms than at the previous stage. SOFT CRACK: the ball will stick to your teeth if you bite it, but doesn't snap or break. HARD CRACK OR CARAMEL: a breakable ball forms, and the sugar is amber-colored.

■ INGREDIENTS

- 2 cups (16 fl oz/500 ml) heavy (double) cream
- 4 tablespoons confectioners' (icing) sugar

Right:
Caramello

Meringa
Meringue

Meringue is made of egg whites whisked as stiffly as possible and mixed with confectioners' (icing) sugar. Meringue can be used to decorate cakes and pies, or cooked and served as individual meringues. A meringue is defined as light if the weight of the sugar is double that of the egg whites, or heavy if the weight of the sugar is three times that of the egg whites. Make sure that no trace of yolk remains in the egg whites. There are two basic ways to make meringue.

Makes: 12 meringues: Preparation: 20 minutes; Cooking: 50-60 minutes; Level of difficulty: Medium

RAW OR COLD METHOD. Add the salt to the egg whites and begin beating them with the electric whisk. § When they begin to stiffen, gradually stir in half the confectioners' sugar. Decrease the speed of the whisk, and gradually add the rest of the sugar. Continue whisking until the mixture is extremely stiff. § Place the mixture in a piping-bag with a plain or fluted nozzle. Line a baking sheet with parchment paper and squeeze out lumps of the mixture, leaving about 2 in (4 cm) between them. § Sprinkle with superfine (caster) sugar and bake in a preheated oven at 250°F/120°C/gas 1 for about 50 minutes. § Baking meringues is a delicate operation. They must dry out without turning brown, so it is a good idea to leave the oven door ajar while they are baking.

HOT MERINGUE MIXTURE. The ingredients and method are the same as for the above recipe, but the egg whites and sugar are combined in a double-boiler and whisked over warm water until very frothy.

■ INGREDIENTS

- dash of salt
- 3 egg whites
- 1½ cups (7 oz/200 g) confectioners' (icing) sugar
- superfine (caster) sugar, for sprinkling on the meringue

Crema inglese
Custard

Egg custard is the simplest of the creamy, egg-based creams used in confectionery. The classic recipe consists of eggs, sugar, and milk. This recipe includes potato starch, which will prevent the custard from curdling. If preferred, use vanilla extract (essence) instead of the vanilla bean.

Makes about 2 cups (16 fl oz/500 ml) custard; Preparation: 10 minutes; Cooking: 10 minutes; Level of difficulty: Simple

Boil the milk with the vanilla bean. § Leave to infuse then remove the bean. § Whisk the egg yolks and sugar until frothy. Stir in the potato flour (potato starch), then gradually add the milk, stirring constantly. § Heat the mixture in the top of a double-boiler over very low heat until thick. Cool quickly in a small bowl over a larger bowl filled with ice and salt.

■ INGREDIENTS

- 2 cups (16 fl oz/500 ml) milk
- 1 vanilla bean
- 5 egg yolks
- ⅓ cup (3 oz/90 g) sugar
- 1 teaspoon potato flour (potato starch)

VARIATION
– The milk may be flavored with lemon zest instead of vanilla.

Right: *Meringa*

ZABAIONE
Zabaione

Zabaione is similar to custard, but the milk is replaced by a dry Marsala wine. The recipe is popular all over Italy. Zabaione is said to have derived its name from San Pasquale Baylon, patron saint of the confectioners of Turin, who dedicated this exquisite preparation to him in the 18th century. However, it appears to have been known to the Court of the Gonzaga family of Mantua as long ago as the second half of the 17th century. Zabaione can be eaten hot or cold, served in a bowl by itself or with fruit or cookies, or used as a filling for cakes and fritters.

Serves: 4; Preparation: 15 minutes; Cooking: 10 minutes; Level of difficulty: Simple

Put the egg yolks and sugar in a heavy-bottomed saucepan and whisk until pale and creamy. § Add the Marsala gradually, still beating, then place the saucepan in a larger pan of hot water over very low heat (or use a double-boiler). Cook, beating all the time with the whisk, until the mixture thickens. Keep the heat very low and never let the zabaione boil or it will curdle. § If serving cold, cover with a layer of plastic wrap so that it touches the surface, to prevent a skin from forming as the mixture cools.

■ INGREDIENTS

- 4 egg yolks
- 4 tablespoons sugar
- 8 tablespoons dry Marsala

CREMA PASTICCERA
Vanilla pastry cream

This is another basic recipe used in confectionery to make desserts and fillings. There are numerous variations of the main ingredients and a variety of liqueurs and other flavorings can be added.

Makes: approximately 2 cups (16 fl oz/500 ml) pastry cream; Preparation: 10 minutes; Cooking: 10 minutes; Level of difficulty: Simple

Whisk the egg yolks and sugar until very pale and creamy. Stir in the flour. § Bring the milk to a boil, then remove from heat. § Stir the egg and flour mixture into the milk, then cook over very low heat, stirring constantly to prevent the mixture from becoming lumpy. § When thick, add the vanilla extract, and pour into a bowl. Cover with a layer of plastic wrap touching the surface to prevent a skin from forming.

■ INGREDIENTS

- 5 egg yolks
- ¾ cup (5 oz/150 g) sugar
- ⅓ cup (1¼ oz/40 g) all-purpose (plain) flour
- 2 cups (16 fl oz/500 ml) milk
- dash of salt
- 2–3 drops vanilla extract (essence)

VARIATIONS
– To make chocolate pastry cream, melt 4 squares (4 oz/125 g) of grated bittersweet (baking) chocolate in the milk and omit the salt.
– To make lemon pastry cream, boil the zest of one lemon in the milk.
– To make hazelnut or almond pastry cream, add 2 tablespoons of ground hazelnuts or almonds to the cream while still hot.
– To make liqueur pastry cream, add one or two tablespoons of rum, cognac, or other liqueur to the cream while still hot.

Right: *Crema pasticcera*

Cakes and Pies

*Despite the wonderful cake shops all over Italy,
home-baked cakes and pies are as popular as ever.
This chapter has a selection of some classic recipes as
well as some personal favorites.*

Torta sbrisolona
Almond polenta cake

This simple but delicious cake is typical Lombardy peasant fare. As the Italian name implies, it crumbles easily; serve it in pieces broken into irregular shapes.

Serves: 4-6; Preparation: 20 minutes; Cooking: 40 minutes; Level of difficulty: Simple

Chop the almonds in a food processor with two-thirds of the superfine sugar. § Transfer to a work surface and add the flour, cornmeal, lemon zest, remaining superfine sugar, vanilla sugar, and salt. Shape into a mound and make a well in the center. § Combine the butter and lard with the egg yolks, and add to the flour mixture. Working quickly, use your fingertips to combine the mixture until it is smooth and crumbly. § Place the dough in a buttered and floured pie dish, 10 in (25 cm) in diameter, pressing down lightly with your fingertips to make an uneven surface. § Bake in a preheated oven at 375°F/190°C/gas 5 for 40 minutes. § If liked, sprinkle with confectioners' (icing) sugar before serving.

VARIATIONS
– Replace the almonds with the same quantity of toasted hazelnuts.
– For a lighter cake, replace the lard with the same quantity of butter.

■ INGREDIENTS

- 1¾ cups (8 oz/250 g) almonds, blanched
- ¾ cup (5 oz/150 g) superfine (caster) sugar
- 2 cups (7 oz/200 g) all-purpose (plain) flour
- 2½ cups (8 oz/250 g) yellow cornmeal, finely ground
- grated zest of 1 lemon
- 1 teaspoon vanilla sugar
- dash of salt
- ½ cup (4 oz/125 g) butter, cut in small pieces
- ⅓ cup (3½ oz/100 g) lard, cut in small pieces
- 2 egg yolks, beaten

Amor polenta
Sweet polenta pie

This is another typical dish from Lombardy, in northern Italy.

Serves: 6-8; Preparation: 30 minutes; Cooking: 40 minutes; Level of difficulty: Medium

Melt the butter and set aside to cool. § Add all but 2 tablespoons of the confectioners' sugar and beat until creamy. § Add the whole eggs, one at a time, and then the yolks, beating continuously with a whisk. § Add the liqueur and almonds and sift in the cornmeal and flour. § Beat for some time, then mix in the baking powder and vanilla sugar. § Pour the mixture into a buttered and floured soufflé dish or fluted mold 6 in (15 cm) in diameter and bake in a preheated oven at 350°F/180°C/gas 4 for about 40 minutes. § Serve sprinkled with the remaining confectioners' sugar.

■ INGREDIENTS

- 1 cup (8 oz/250 g) butter
- 2 cups (14 oz/400 g) confectioners' (icing) sugar
- 3 whole eggs and 6 egg yolks
- 2 tablespoons Strega liqueur (or dark rum)
- 1⅓ cups (5½ oz/170 g) almonds, ground
- 1¾ cups (7 oz/200 g) yellow cornmeal, coarsely ground
- 1¼ cups (5 oz/150 g) all-purpose (plain) flour
- 2 teaspoons baking powder
- 1 teaspoon vanilla sugar

Right: *Torta sbrisolona*

Torta di riso
Rice tart

Serves: 6; Preparation: 10 minutes + time to make the pastry; Cooking: 1¼ hours; Level of difficulty: Medium

Prepare the pastry. § Cook the rice in the milk with a little salt for about 30 minutes. § When the milk has been completely absorbed, remove from heat, then add the superfine sugar and mix well. Set aside to cool. § Add the egg yolks one at a time, then the raisins, lemon zest, and rum. § Beat the egg whites with a dash of salt until stiff, and fold them into the mixture. § Line a buttered and floured pie dish 10 in (25 cm) in diameter with the pastry, reserving some for decoration. Leave a raised edge about 1 in (2.5 cm) high, pinching the edges to make it look attractive. Prick the base with a fork to stop the pastry puffing up during baking. § Carefully pour in the rice mixture. § Cut the reserved pastry into strips or shapes and use to decorate the top. § Bake in a preheated oven at 350°F/180°C/gas 4 for about 40 minutes.

Variation
– Mix about half the rice mixture with 3 tablespoons of cocoa powder. Pour the chocolate rice into the pie dish over the pastry and cover with the white mixture for a two-tone pie.

■ INGREDIENTS
- 1 quantity *Sweet plain pastry* (see recipe p. 10)
- 1¼ cups (8 oz/250 g) short-grain rice (preferably arborio)
- 4 cups (32 fl oz/1 liter) milk
- dash of salt
- ½ cup (3½ oz/100 g) superfine (caster) sugar
- 4 eggs, separated
- ⅓ cup (2 oz/60 g) raisins
- 1 tablespoon lemon zest, grated
- 1 tablespoon dark rum

Torta della nonna
Grandmother's pie

This is one of the most popular and delicious desserts in the Italian repertoire.

Serves: 6; Preparation: 30 minutes; Cooking: 40 minutes + time to make the cream; Level of difficulty: Medium

Cream the butter and superfine sugar and then beat in the eggs. Add the flour and baking powder and mix well. § Divide the dough in half and roll out into two rounds. § Place one in a buttered and floured pie dish 10 in (25 cm) in diameter, and cover with the pastry cream, piling it slightly higher in the center. § Cover with the other round and seal the edges together. § Bake in a preheated oven at 350°F/180°C/gas 4 for about 40 minutes. When the pie is cooked, decorate with the slivered almonds and sprinkle with the confectioners' sugar.

Variation
– Replace *Vanilla pastry cream* with *Chocolate pastry cream* (see recipe page 20).

■ INGREDIENTS
- ½ cup (4 oz/125 g) butter
- ⅔ cup (4 oz /125 g) superfine (caster) sugar
- 2 eggs
- 2½ cups (8 oz/250 g) all-purpose (plain) flour, sifted
- 1 teaspoon baking powder
- dash of salt
- 1 quantity *Vanilla pastry cream* (see recipe p. 20)
- 2 tablespoons almonds, slivered (flaked)
- confectioners' (icing) sugar for sprinkling

Right:
Torta della nonna

Torta Roberta
Fresh fruit cake

Serves: 6; Preparation: 10 minutes; Cooking: 30 minutes; Level of difficulty: Simple

Beat the eggs and superfine sugar, then add the butter, salt, and sifted flour and, lastly, the baking powder and water. § Mix to a smooth cream. § Stir the fruit into the mixture. § Pour into a buttered and floured springform pan 8 in (20 cm) in diameter and bake in a preheated oven at 350°F/180°C/gas 4 for 30 minutes.

VARIATION
– This cake can be varied infinitely, depending on the fruit used. Try it with bananas, apricots, and pitted (stoned) cherries.

■ INGREDIENTS

- 2 eggs
- 4 tablespoons superfine (caster) sugar
- ½ cup (4 oz/125 g) butter, melted
- dash of salt
- 4 tablespoons all-purpose (plain) flour
- 1 teaspoon baking powder
- 2 tablespoons water
- 1 pear, 1 apple, 1 peach, peeled, cored, and chopped into tiny pieces

■ INGREDIENTS

- ¾ cup (7½ oz/225 g) butter
- ½ cup (3½ oz/100 g) superfine (caster) sugar
- 2 eggs
- 2½ cups (8 oz/250 g) all-purpose (plain) flour
- 2 teaspoons baking powder
- dash of cinnamon, ground
- 1 cup (8 fl oz/250 ml) yogurt
- grated zest of 1 lemon
- ¾ cup (7 oz/200 g) chocolate hazelnut paste

TOPPING:
- 2 tablespoons all-purpose (plain) flour
- 2 tablespoons butter
- 2½ tablespoons superfine (caster) sugar
- 1 cup (3½ oz/100 g) hazelnuts, toasted and coarsely chopped
- ⅓ cup (3½ fl oz/100 ml) heavy (double) cream

■ INGREDIENTS

- 1½ quantities *Italian sponge cake* (see recipe p. 14)
- 1 quantity *Vanilla pastry cream* (see recipe p. 20)
- ½ cup (4 fl oz/125 ml) Grand Marnier
- ½ cup (3½ oz/100 g) superfine (caster) sugar
- ¾ cup (7 fl oz/200 ml) water

Torta alla crema Gianduia
Hazelnut cream pie

Hazelnut and chocolate cream, known as Gianduia *in Italian, is typical of traditional Piedmontese baking.*

Serves: 6; Preparation: 20 minutes; Cooking: 45 minutes; Level of difficulty: Medium

Cream the first measure of butter and superfine sugar and then beat in the eggs. § Stir in the first measure of flour, the baking powder, and cinnamon, and then add all but 2 tablespoons of the yogurt, and the lemon zest. Mix until smooth. § Pour half the mixture into a buttered and floured pie dish 10 in (25 cm) in diameter. § Spread the chocolate hazelnut paste over the base and cover with the remaining dough. § Combine the remaining flour, butter, and superfine sugar with the nuts, until the mixture resembles coarse bread crumbs. § Sprinkle this over the pie and bake in a preheated oven at 350°F/180°C/gas 4 for about 45 minutes. § Whip the cream with the remaining yogurt and serve with the pie.

Torta mimosa
Mimosa cake

Serves: 6-8; Preparation: 10 minutes + time to make the sponge cake and pastry cream; Level of difficulty: Medium

Prepare the sponge cake and the pastry cream. § When the sponge has cooled, cut it crosswise into three layers, one slightly thinner than the others. § Carefully cut the outer crust off the thinnest layer and either crumble it into large crumbs or cut into tiny cubes. § Mix the Grand Marnier with the sugar and water and soak one of the thick layers in this. Spread with some of the pastry cream, mounding it up slightly in the center. § Cover with the remaining layer of sponge cake and spread the remaining pastry cream over the top and sides. § Finally, sprinkle the cake with the crumbs or tiny cubes to achieve the classic mimosa effect.

Left:
Torta mimosa

VARIATION
– Replace the Grand Marnier with pineapple juice and mix finely-chopped pieces of canned pineapple into the pastry cream.

Torta alle nocciole
Hazelnut cake

*This cake is a gourmet's delight. The combination
of chocolate, nuts, and cream is irresistible.*

Serves: 6; Preparation: 40 minutes; Cooking: 50 minutes; Level of difficulty: Complicated

Cream the butter and brown sugar and then beat in the egg yolks one at a time. § Stir in the sifted flour and baking powder. § Add the nuts and chocolate. § Beat the egg whites with the salt until stiff and fold them into the mixture. § Pour the mixture into a buttered and floured springform pan 10 in (25 cm) in diameter, and bake in a preheated oven at 350°F/180°C/gas 4 for about 50 minutes. § Remove from the pan and place on a rack to cool. § Melt the chocolate in a double boiler. Use a wooden spoon to stir in the vanilla. § Whip the cream until stiff. § When the cake is cool, split it into two layers. § Sandwich the cake together with whipped cream and cover with the chocolate frosting. § Decorate with the hazelnuts.

VARIATION
– Stir a handful of chocolate chips into the cream for the filling.

Torta alla crema moka
Mocha cream cake

This cream-filled cake is the classic combination of coffee and chocolate.

Serves: 6; Preparation: 30 minutes; Cooking: 45 minutes; Level of difficulty: Medium

Cream the egg yolks and superfine sugar thoroughly using a whisk. § Stir in the milk, melted butter, cocoa, coffee, sifted flour, baking powder, and salt. § Beat the egg whites until stiff and fold them into the mixture. § Pour the mixture into a buttered and floured springform pan 10 in (25 cm) in diameter, and bake in a preheated oven at 350°F/180°C/gas 4 for about 30 minutes. § Remove from the pan and place on a rack to cool. § Prepare the pastry cream. § Dissolve the gelatin in the hot coffee and stir well. § Mix the coffee and gelatin into the pastry cream. § Slice the cooled cake crosswise in 2 rounds, and fill with the pastry cream. § Whip the cream with the cinnamon and spread it over the cake.

■ INGREDIENTS

- ⅔ cup (5 oz/150 g) butter, cut into pieces
- ¾ cup (5 oz/150 g) brown sugar
- 4 eggs, separated
- 1 cup (3½ oz/100 g) all-purpose (plain) flour
- 1 teaspoon baking powder
- 1 cup (3½ oz/100 g) hazelnuts, toasted and chopped
- 7 squares (7 oz/200 g) semi-sweet (dark) chocolate, chopped
- dash of salt
FROSTING:
- 5½ squares (5½ oz/165 g) semi-sweet (dark) chocolate
- 2–3 drops vanilla extract (essence)
- 2 tablespoons light (single) cream
FILLING:
- ½ cup (4 fl oz/125 ml) heavy (double) cream
DECORATION:
- 2 tablespoons hazelnuts, chopped

■ INGREDIENTS

- 4 eggs, separated
- ¾ cup (5 oz/150 g) superfine (caster) sugar
- ⅓ cup (3½ fl oz/100 ml) milk
- 1 cup (8 oz/250 g) butter, melted
- 2 tablespoons unsweetened cocoa powder
- 2 tablespoons instant coffee powder
- 2½ cups (8 oz/250 g) all-purpose (plain) flour
- 1 teaspoon baking powder
- dash of salt
- 1 quantity *Vanilla pastry cream* (see recipe p. 20)
- ⅓ cup (3½ fl oz/100 ml) strong hot coffee
- 2 tablespoons gelatin
- ¾ cup (7 fl oz/200 ml) heavy (double) cream
- dash of cinnamon

Right: Torta alle nocciole

Torta con ghiaccia
Lemon cake

Serves: 6: Preparation: 20 minutes; Cooking: 60 minutes; Level of difficulty: Simple

Beat the butter and lemon rind until fluffy, then beat in the superfine sugar and eggs alternately. § Stir in the two flours and the baking powder. § Pour the mixture into a buttered and floured loaf pan 8 x 3½ in (20 x 9 cm) in size, and bake in a preheated oven at 350°F/180°C/gas 4 for about 1 hour. § Beat the confectioners' sugar with enough lemon juice to make a stiff frosting. § Frost the cake while it is still hot.

■ INGREDIENTS

- ¾ cup (7½ oz/225 g) butter
- grated zest of 1 lemon
- 1¼ cups (8 oz/250 g) superfine (caster) sugar
- 4 eggs
- 1 generous cup (4 oz/125 g) potato starch (potato flour)
- 1 generous cup (4 oz/125 g) all-purpose (plain) flour
- ½ teaspoon baking powder

FROSTING:
- 1¼ cups (5 oz/150 g) confectioners' (icing) sugar
- 4 tablespoons lemon juice

Torta di mele caramellate
Caramel apple pie

Serves: 6; Preparation: 45 minutes + resting time for the dough; Cooking: 40 minutes; Level of difficulty: Medium

Prepare the short crust pastry. § Peel and dice the apples. § Melt the butter, then add the apples and cook with the lemon juice and half the brown sugar until slightly softened. § Roll out the dough and use it to line a springform pan 10 in (25 cm) in diameter. § Prick the base with a fork and bake in a preheated oven at 350°F/180°C/gas 4 for 30 minutes. § Spread the pastry cream over the pastry and cover with the cooked apples. § Sprinkle with the remaining brown sugar and place the pie under the broiler (grill) until the sugar caramelizes over the apples.

VARIATION
– This delicious pie is also very good when made with pears.

■ INGREDIENTS

- 1 quantity *Plain sweet pastry* (see recipe p. 10)
- 2 lb (1 kg) Golden Delicious apples
- ⅓ cup (3½ oz/100 g) butter
- juice of ½ lemon
- ¾ cup (5 oz/150 g) brown sugar
- ½ quantity *Vanilla pastry cream* (see recipe p. 20)

Right:
Torta di mele caramellate

Quattro quarti al cioccolato
Four quarters with chocolate

Serves: 4-6; Preparation: 20 minutes; Cooking: 40 minutes; Level of difficulty: Simple

Beat the egg yolks and superfine sugar until the mixture is creamy. § Add the melted butter, followed by the sifted flour, cocoa, vanilla extract, and baking powder. § Whisk the egg whites with the salt until very stiff and fold them into the dough. § Tip the mixture into a buttered and floured square pan 8 in (20 cm) in length, and bake in a preheated oven at 350°F/180°C/gas 4 for about 40 minutes. § When cool, cover the cake with the melted chocolate and decorate with chocolate shavings.

VARIATION
– The traditional recipe uses 1 cup (3½ oz/100 g) ground almonds instead of unsweetened cocoa.

■ INGREDIENTS

- 3 eggs, separated
- ¾ cup (5 oz/150 g) superfine (caster) sugar
- ¾ cup (7½ oz/225 g) butter, melted
- 2 cups (7 oz/200 g) all-purpose (plain) flour
- 2 tablespoons unsweetened cocoa powder
- 2–3 drops vanilla extract (essence)
- 1 teaspoon baking powder
- dash of salt

FROSTING:

- 7 squares (7 oz/200 g) semi-sweet (dark) chocolate, melted
- chocolate shavings to decorate

Sfogliata di arance
Orange puff

The caramelized sugar contrasts perfectly with the tangy flavor of the oranges.

Serves: 6; Preparation: about 1 hour; Cooking: 30 minutes; Level of difficulty: Complicated

Cream the butter and brown sugar and spread it over the bottom of a 10 in (25 cm) pie dish lined with dampened baking parchment (paper). Chill in the refrigerator. § Remove the dish from the refrigerator, then cut the orange into very thin slices and arrange them on the butter-and-sugar base so that they overlap one another slightly. § Cover with a round of thinly rolled puff pastry. Prick the surface with a fork and bake in a preheated oven at 350°F/180°C/gas 4 for about 30 minutes. § When baked, turn out onto a serving dish. Remove the parchment carefully and serve. § If the surface is not well caramelized, place the pie under the grill (broiler) for a few minutes.

VARIATION
– This pie is equally delicious made with apples.

■ INGREDIENTS

- 4 tablespoons butter
- 4 tablespoons brown sugar
- 1 large orange
- ¼ quantity *Puff pastry* (see recipe p. 12)

Right: Sfogliata di arance

TORTA DI GRANO SARACENO
Buckwheat cake

This cake comes from the Dolomite mountains, where buckwheat is cultivated in the deep valleys. Buckwheat flour is used in many regional dishes and country desserts.

Serves: 8; Preparation: 20 minutes; Cooking: 60 minutes; Level of difficulty: simple

Cream the butter and superfine sugar and then add the egg yolks one at a time. § Add the flour, almonds, and vanilla extract and beat until smooth. § Beat the egg whites with the salt until stiff. Fold them into the mixture. § Pour into a buttered and floured pie dish 10 in (25 cm) in diameter, and bake in a preheated oven at 350°F/180°C/gas 4 for about 60 minutes. § Remove the cake from the oven and leave to cool on a rack. § Slice it crosswise into 2 rounds. Sandwich the rounds together with the redcurrant jelly and sprinkle the top with vanilla sugar.

VARIATION
– Serve with lightly whipped, unsweetened cream.

■ INGREDIENTS

- 1 cup (8 oz/250 g) butter
- 1¼ cups (8 oz/250 g) superfine (caster) sugar
- 6 eggs, separated
- 1½ cups (8 oz/250 g) buckwheat flour
- 2 cups (8 oz/250 g) almonds, chopped
- 2–3 drops vanilla extract (essence)
- dash of salt
- 1¼ cups (13 oz/400 g) redcurrant jelly (jam)
- 1 tablespoon vanilla sugar

TORTA DI PATATE
Potato cake

This simple cake has a mild flavor, which makes it particularly popular with children.

Serves: 6; Preparation: 40 minutes; Cooking: 40 minutes; Level of difficulty: Simple

Boil the potatoes in their skins until tender. Slip off the skins and mash while still warm. § Combine the sifted flour with the baking powder and lemon rind. § Mix the potatoes with the Ricotta, superfine sugar, butter, and eggs. § Combine the flour and potato mixtures, and mix until smooth. Place in a buttered and floured springform pan 10 in (25 cm) in diameter. § Bake in a preheated oven at 350°F/180°C/gas 4 for about 40 minutes. Serve sprinkled with vanilla sugar.

VARIATION
– Flavor the cake with grated orange zest instead of lemon zest.

■ INGREDIENTS

- 4 large potatoes
- 2 cups (7 oz/200 g) all-purpose (plain) flour
- 1 tablespoon baking powder
- 1 teaspoon grated lemon zest
- 1⅔ cups (13 oz/400 g) Ricotta cheese
- 1⅓ cups (10 oz/300 g) superfine (caster) sugar
- 4 tablespoons butter, melted
- 4 eggs
- 2 tablespoons vanilla sugar

Right:
Torta di grano saraceno

INGREDIENTS

- 2 eggs
- 1 cup (7 oz/200 g) superfine (caster) sugar
- 2½ cups (8 oz/250 g) finely ground cornmeal
- 2 cups (8 oz/250 g) all-purpose (plain) flour
- 2 teaspoons baking powder
- ⅔ cup (5 fl oz/150 ml) oil
- ½ cup (4 fl oz/125 ml) white wine
- 1 apple
- juice of half a lemon
- 2 tablespoons superfine (caster) sugar

TORTA DI FARINA GIALLA E MELE
Cornmeal and apple cake

Serves: 6. Preparation: 20 minutes; Cooking: about 50 minutes; Level of difficulty: Simple

Cream the butter and eggs § Stir in the sifted cornmeal and flour, then add the baking powder. § Pour in the oil in a thin stream, then add the wine. § When the dough is smooth and creamy, pour it into a buttered and floured springform pan 9 in (23 cm) in diameter. § Peel and core the apple and slice it thinly. Sprinkle it with the lemon juice. § Arrange the slices over the cake and sprinkle with the sugar. Bake in a preheated oven at 350°F/180°C/gas 4 for 50 minutes.

■ INGREDIENTS

- ½ cup (4 oz/125 g) butter
- ½ cup (3½ oz/100 g) superfine (caster) sugar
- grated zest of 1 lemon
- 2 eggs
- dash of salt
- 2½ cups (8 oz/250 g) all-purpose (plain) flour
- ⅓ cup (3½ fl oz/100 ml) milk
- 2 teaspoons baking powder
- 4 medium cooking apples
- 2 tablespoons lemon juice
- 2 tablespoons apricot jelly (jam)

TORTA DI MELE RUSTICA
Country apple cake

Serves: 6; Preparation time: 30 minutes; Cooking time: 45 minutes; Level of difficulty: Simple

Cream the butter and superfine sugar together with the lemon zest. § Beat in the eggs, one at a time, followed by the salt and sifted flour, alternating them with the milk. Fold in the baking powder. § Place the dough in a buttered and floured pie dish 10 in (25 cm) in diameter. § Peel the apples, cut them in half, and core. Cut a grid pattern into the rounded sides, and sprinkle with lemon juice. § Place the apples, flat side down, in the top of the cake. § Bake in a preheated oven at 350°F/180°C/gas 4 for about 45 minutes. § When the cake is cooked, spread the top with a little of the warmed, strained apricot jelly and serve.

■ INGREDIENTS

- 1¼ cups (8 oz/250 g) superfine (caster) sugar
- 1¾ cups (8 oz/250 g) almonds, toasted
- 3 eggs
- ⅓ cup (3½ oz/100 g) butter, melted
- dash of salt
- ¾ cup (3 oz/90 g) all-purpose (plain) flour
- extra superfine (caster) sugar for the pan

CIAMBELLA AL CARAMELLO
Praline savarin

Serves: 6; Preparation: 35 minutes; Cooking: 35 minutes; Level of Difficulty: Medium

Place the sugar in a dry, , heavy-bottomed pan and cook lightly until it turns an amber color. Place on a sheet of baking parchment (paper) and leave to cool. § When the caramelized sugar is cold, grind it in a food processor with the toasted almonds. § Beat the eggs in a bowl. Gradually beat in the caramel and almond mixture. Slowly add the butter, salt, and sifted flour. § Turn the mixture into a buttered and sugared savarin or bundt pan about 9½ in (24 cm) in diameter, and bake in a preheated oven at 350°/180°C/gas 4 for about 35 minutes.

VARIATION
— When making the caramel, a tablespoon of honey can be added to the sugar.

Left:
Torta di mele rustica

TORTA AL LIMONE
Lemon pie

This delicately flavored, slightly sharp-tasting pie is perfect for teatime.

Serves: 6; Preparation: 45 minutes + time for the pastry to rest; Cooking: 40 minutes; Level of difficulty: Medium

Prepare the short crust pastry and use it to line a buttered and floured pie dish 10 in (25 cm) in diameter. Prick the base of the pie all over with a fork. § Beat the eggs and sugar in a bowl with the ground almonds, egg whites, melted butter, and the juice and rind of the lemons. § Spread this mixture over the dough and bake in a preheated oven at 350°F/180°C/gas 4 for about 40 minutes. § Decorate the pie with the candied peel and sprinkle with a little confectioners' sugar. Serve chilled.

VARIATION
– Cover with a layer of meringue, as in the recipe on page 50.

■ INGREDIENTS

- 1 quantity *Short crust pastry* (see recipe p. 10), made with sugar
- 2 eggs
- 1 cup (7 oz/200 g) superfine (caster) sugar
- 2 cups (7 oz/200 g) almonds, ground
- 2 egg whites
- ⅓ cup (3½ oz/100 g) butter, melted
- grated zest and juice of 2 lemons
- 10 pieces candied lemon peel
- confectioners' (icing) sugar for sprinkling

STRUDEL DI MELE
Apple strudel

This dessert is made throughout central Europe. In Italy, it is popular in the northeast — in Trentino, Alto Adige, and Venezia Giulia.

Serves: 4-6; Preparation: 30 minutes + 30 minutes for the dough to rest; Cooking: 60 minutes; Level of difficulty: Complicated

Heat the water and melt the butter in it. Leave to cool. § Sift the flour onto a work surface and shape into a mound. Make a well in the center and fill with salt, sugar, egg, and butter-and-water mixture. § Combine the ingredients well and knead vigorously for 20 minutes, until it forms a soft, elastic dough. Roll into a ball. Cover and leave in a warm place to rest for about 30 minutes. § Meanwhile, peel and core the apples and slice thinly. § Leave the raisins to soften in warm water for 10 minutes. § Mix the sugar with the cinnamon and lemon zest. § Toast the bread crumbs in half the butter. § At this point, place the dough on a large, floured cloth and roll it out partially with a rolling-pin. Then try to stretch it out as much as possible, placing your fists underneath the dough with your knuckles upward and pulling gently outward from the center. The dough should be almost as thin as a sheet of paper. § Brush

■ INGREDIENTS

- ⅓ cup (3½ fl oz/100 ml) water
- 4 tablespoons butter
- 2½ cups (8 oz/250 g) all-purpose (plain) flour
- dash of salt
- 1 teaspoon superfine (caster) sugar
- 1 egg

FILLING:

- 8 russet apples
- ⅔ cup (4 oz/125 g) raisins
- ⅓ cup (3 oz/90 g) superfine (caster) sugar
- ½ teaspoon cinnamon, ground
- grated zest of 1 lemon

Right:
Strudel di mele

- 1¼ cups (5 oz/150 g) dry white bread crumbs
- ⅓ cup (3½ oz/100 g) butter
- ⅓ cup (3½ oz/100 g) apricot jelly
- confectioners' (icing) sugar for sprinkling

it with melted butter. Sprinkle half the dough with the bread crumbs, followed by the apples, raisins, and sugar mixture. Spread with the apricot jelly, which serves to bind the mixture. § Roll up the strudel carefully, sealing the edges well so that no filling will escape during cooking. Place on a baking sheet covered in baking parchment (paper). § Brush with melted butter and bake in a preheated oven at 350°F/180°C/gas 4 for about 1 hour. Serve sprinkled with confectioners' sugar.

VARIATION
– Try substituting 3½ cups (1¾ lb/800 g) morello cherries and slivered (flaked) almonds for the apples and raisins. This is delicious served with lightly whipped cream.

Torta di ricotta al frutti di bosco
Ricotta cake with fruits of the forest

Serves: 6; Preparation: 40 minutes + time to chill; Level of difficulty: Medium

Combine the Ricotta with just over half the superfine sugar and the yogurt in a mixing bowl. § Whip the cream until stiff and fold it carefully into the mixture. § Lastly, stir in 3 tablespoons of berries. § Place a sponge cake round in the bottom of a cake pan 10 in (25 cm) in diameter and spread the Ricotta mixture over it. Cover with the other piece of sponge. § Cook the rest of the berries in the remaining sugar and lemon juice over a high heat until syrupy. § Spread the fruit over the the cake and refrigerate for at least 3 hours before serving.

VARIATION
– Buy the sponge cake ready-made to save time.

■ INGREDIENTS

• 2 cups (1 lb/500 g) Ricotta cheese, strained
• 1¼ cups (8 oz/250 g) superfine (caster) sugar
• 1 cup (8 fl oz/250 ml) Greek yogurt
• 1¾ cups (14 fl oz/ 450 ml) heavy (double) cream
• 2 cups (1 lb/500 g) mixed berry fruits
• 2 quantities *Italian sponge cake* (see recipe p. 14), baked in two round pans 8 in (20 cm) in diameter
• juice of 1 lemon

Schiacciata alla fiorentina
Florentine cake

*In Florence this dish is traditionally
eaten on the Thursday before Lent.
It is delicious when filled with whipped cream.*

Serves: 8; Preparation: 30 minutes + 3 hours to rise; Cooking: 30 minutes; Level of difficulty: Medium

Dissolve the yeast in a quarter of the warm water. Set aside for 10–15 minutes. § Place the flour in a large mixing bowl and pour in the yeast mixture. Stir until well mixed. Turn out onto a floured work surface and knead mixture vigorously until the dough is smooth and elastic. Roll into a ball. Cover and leave in a warm place to rise for about 1 hour. § Knead the dough again, then gradually work in the eggs, sugar, butter, orange rind, and salt. § Spread the dough in a buttered and floured 8 x 12 in (20 x 30 cm) baking dish, and leave to rise for 2 more hours. § Bake in a preheated oven at 350°F/180°C/gas 4 for about 30 minutes. When cool, sprinkle with confectioners' sugar and serve.

■ INGREDIENTS

• ½ oz (15 g) fresh yeast or 1 (¼ oz/7.5 g) package active dry yeast
• 1 cup (8 fl oz/250 ml)
• 4 cups (1 lb/500 g) all-purpose (plain) flour
• 4 egg yolks
• ¾ cup (5 oz/150 g) superfine (caster) sugar
• ⅓ cup (3½ oz/100 g) butter, melted
• grated zest of 1 orange
• dash of salt
• vanilla sugar
• confectioners' (icing) sugar for sprinkling

Right:
Torta di ricotta ai frutti di bosco

CROSTATA ALLA CREMA DI AMARENE
Cherry cream pie

Serves: 6; Preparation: 20 minutes + time to make the pastry and pastry cream; Cooking: about 1 hour; Level of difficulty: Simple

Prepare the pastry. Use it to line a pie dish 9 in (23 cm) in diameter. Bake blind, following the method on page 10. § Let the pastry shell cool and then spread evenly with the pastry cream. § Arrange the cherries over the cream and place under a very hot broiler (grill) for about 10 minutes. § Sprinkle with confectioners' sugar and serve while still warm.

SCHIACCIATA ALL'UVA
Grape bread

This recipe for sweet focaccia comes from Tuscany, where it is made every year throughout the grape harvest using the small black grapes used to make the local Chianti wines.

Serves: 6-8; Preparation: 40 minutes + time for the dough to rise; Cooking: 45-50 minutes; Level of difficulty: Medium

Dissolve the yeast in a third of the warm water. Set aside for 10–15 minutes. § Sift the flour onto a work surface and add the superfine sugar and salt. Shape into a mound and make a well in the center. Pour in the yeast mixture and work it into the flour. Knead vigorously, until the dough is soft and elastic. Roll into a ball. Cover and leave in a warm place to rise until it has doubled in size. § Divide the risen dough in two. Roll out two sheets about ¾ in (2 cm) thick. Place one of these on a buttered baking sheet and cover it with half the grapes and half the sugar. Place the other sheet on top and seal the edges thoroughly. § Spread the remainder of the grapes over the top, pressing them down into the dough. Sprinkle with the sugar and leave to rest for 1 hour. § Bake in a preheated oven at 350°F/180°C/gas 4 for 40–50 minutes.

VARIATION
– For extra flavor, fry a sprig of rosemary in 2 tablespoonfuls of extra-virgin olive oil. Strain the rosemary leaves from the oil then work it into the dough.

Left:
Crostata alla crema di amarene

La crostata della zia Ines
Cherry jelly pie

Serves: 6; Preparation: 45 minutes; Cooking: 30 minutes; Level of difficulty: Simple

Beat the whole egg and the yolks with the sugar until pale and creamy. Add the butter and mix well. § Sift the flour and stir it into the egg mixture together with the Maraschino, lemon zest, and baking powder. § When the dough is well mixed, cover the mixing bowl with a cloth and set aside to rest for 30 minutes. § Line a buttered and floured pie dish 10 in (25 cm) in diameter with two-thirds of the pastry, pressing it down with your fingertips. Prick the bottom of the pie with a fork. Spread the cherry jelly over the pastry. § Roll out the remaining pastry and cut into strips. Use them to make a lattice pattern on the top of the pie. § Bake in a preheated oven at 350°F/180°C/gas 4 for 30 minutes.

VARIATION
– Replace the cherry jelly with the same quantity of plum, blackberry, or apricot jelly.

■ INGREDIENTS

- 1 egg
- 2 egg yolks
- ⅓ cup (3 oz/90 g) superfine (caster) sugar
- ⅔ cup (5 oz/ 150 g) butter, melted
- 3 cups (10½ oz/300 g) all-purpose (plain) flour
- 1 tablespoon Maraschino liqueur (cherry liqueur)
- grated zest of 1 lemon
- 1 teaspoon baking powder,
- 1 cup cherry jelly (jam)

Crostata di uva
Grape pie

Grapes, almonds, and sweet plain pastry — three simple ingredients to make a sophisticated dessert.

Serves: 6; Preparation: 30 minutes; Cooking: 30 minutes; Level of difficulty: Simple

Make the pastry, working half the ground almonds into the dough. Set aside to rest for 30 minutes. § Roll out the dough and use it to line a pie dish 10 in (25 cm) in diameter. § Sauté the grapes in the butter for 5 minutes. § Increase the heat to high and add the brown sugar and rum. Stir well and remove from heat. § Scatter the Amaretti cookies over the pastry shell, then add the grapes and all their juice. § Sprinkle with the remaining ground almonds and bake in a preheated oven at 350°F/180°C/gas 4 for about 30 minutes.

VARIATION
– Replace the grapes with an equal quantity of apples, pears, or plums.

■ INGREDIENTS

- 1 quantity *Sweet plain pastry* (see recipe p. 10)
- 1 cup (3½ oz/100 g) almonds, ground
- 3 cups (1½ lb/750 g) white grapes, halved
- 1 tablespoon butter
- 1 tablespoon brown sugar
- 1 tablespoon dark rum
- 5 Amaretti cookies (macaroons), crushed

Right:
La crostata della zia Ines

PASTIERA NAPOLETANA
Neapolitan Ricotta pie

The traditional recipe calls for lard in the pastry base. For a lighter dish, replace with the same quantity of butter. You may also replace the wheat with the same quantity of cooked rice.

Serves: 8; Preparation: 2 hours; Cooking: 1½ hours; Level of difficulty: Medium

Prepare the pastry and set aside to chill. § Cook the cracked wheat, milk, and butter for about 10 minutes, stirring constantly, then set aside to cool. § Beat the eggs and egg yolks into the Ricotta one at a time, then add the sugar, cinnamon, and orange flower water. § Stir in the wheat mixture. § Sprinkle the candied peel with flour and stir it into the filling. § Line a pan 12 in (30 cm) in diameter with two-thirds of the pastry so that it overlaps the edges a little. § Spread with the filling. Roll out the remaining pastry and cut into strips. Use them to make a lattice pattern on the top of the pie. § Bake in a preheated oven at 350°F/180°C/gas 4 for 1½ hours. § Cool for 10 minutes. Sprinkle with confectioners' (icing) sugar and serve.

■ INGREDIENTS

- 2 quantities *Sweet plain pastry* (see recipe p. 10), made with 2 extra whole eggs
- 4 tablespoons cracked wheat, cooked
- ¾ cup (7 fl oz/200 ml) milk
- 4 tablespoons butter
- 7 whole eggs and 3 yolks
- ¾ cup (7 oz/200 g) fresh Ricotta cheese
- 2¼ cups (1 lb/500 g) superfine (caster) sugar
- dash of cinnamon
- 2 tablespoons orange flower water
- ¾ cup (3 oz/90 g) candied lemon peel, chopped
- confectioners' (icing) sugar for sprinkling

CROSTATA DI FRAGOLINE
Wild strawberry pie

The dough for this pie is simply Short crust pastry *(see recipe page 10) in which the water is replaced by milk. The wild strawberries give it a slightly sharp taste plus an exquisite fragrance.*

Serves: 6-8; Preparation: 30 minutes; Cooking: 1 hour; Level of difficulty: Simple

Use the first seven ingredients listed to prepare the short crust pastry, following the method on page 10. Use the pastry to line a cake pan 10 in (25 cm) in diameter. Bake blind in a preheated oven, following the method on page 10. § Beat the eggs with the sugar and add the cream, ground almonds, and flour. § Remove the pastry shell from the oven and cover with the wild strawberries. Pour the egg and cream mixture over the top. § Bake for another 35 minutes.

VARIATION
– Sprinkle the pie with vanilla sugar just before serving.

■ INGREDIENTS

- 2½ cups (8 oz/250 g) all-purpose (plain) flour
- 4 tablespoons superfine (caster) sugar
- ½ cup (4 oz/125 g) butter
- 3 tablespoons milk
- dash of salt

FILLING:

- 2 eggs
- ⅓ cup (3 oz/90 g) superfine (caster) sugar
- ⅓ cup (3½ fl oz/100 ml) light (single) cream
- 1 cup (3½ oz/100 g) almonds, ground
- 2 tablespoons all-purpose (plain) flour
- 1 cup (8 oz/250 g) wild strawberries

Right: *Crostata di fragoline*

Crostata meringata
Meringue pie

■ INGREDIENTS

• 1 quantity *Sweet plain pastry* (see recipe p. 10)
• 1 quantity *Vanilla pastry cream* (see recipe p. 20)
• 4 egg whites
• dash of salt

Serves: 4-6; Preparation: 45 minutes; Cooking: 30 minutes; Level of difficulty: Simple

Prepare the pastry and bake it blind, following the instructions on page 10. § Prepare the pastry cream and pour it into the baked pastry shell. § Beat the egg whites with the salt until very stiff. Spread over the top of the pie, drawing it up into little peaks using the back of a tablespoon. § Return to the oven for about 10 minutes or until the meringue is golden brown.

VARIATION
– Add extra flavor to the vanilla pastry cream by boiling the zest of a lemon in the milk.

Millefoglie di meringa
Meringue mille-feuilles

This is a variation of the classic meringue dessert with cream, but with the addition of lemon-flavored custard.

■ INGREDIENTS

• 4 egg whites
• dash of salt
• ¾ cup (4 oz/125 g) confectioners' (icing) sugar
• ½ cup (3½ oz/100 g) superfine (caster) sugar
FILLING:
• 3 egg yolks
• ½ cup (3½ oz/100 g) superfine (caster) sugar
• 1 tablespoon potato starch (potato flour)
• ⅓ cup (3½ fl oz/100 ml) lemon juice
• 1¼ cups (10 fl oz/300 ml) heavy (double) cream, whipped

Serves: 4-6; Preparation: 40 minutes; Cooking: 40 minutes; Level of difficulty: Complicated

Using an electric whisk, beat the egg whites with the salt until stiff, adding half of both sugars at the beginning and the rest bit by bit, gradually reducing the speed. § Spread the mixture on 2 large baking sheets in 3 disks about 8 in (20 cm) in diameter. § Bake in a preheated oven at 250°F/120°C/gas 1 for about 40 minutes. § To make the filling: beat the egg yolks and the sugar until the mixture falls in ribbons from the beater. § Add the potato starch and place over heat in the top of a double-boiler. § Whisk continuously, slowly adding the lemon juice. Stir over very low heat until the mixture thickens. § Leave to cool before folding in the whipped cream. § Spread half the mixture on top of two disks of meringue. Place one one on top of the other and cover with the third disk. § Serve sprinkled with confectioners' sugar, if liked.

VARIATION
– Subsitute the filling with 1 quantity of *Custard* (see recipe on p. 18) and put flakes of semi-sweet chocolate between the layers.

Right:
Crostata meringata

INGREDIENTS

- ½ quantity *Puff pastry* (see recipe p. 12)
- 1 cup (4 oz/125 g) confectioners' (icing) sugar
- 1 quantity *Zabaione* (see recipe p. 20)
- 1 cup (8 fl oz/250 ml) heavy (double) cream, whipped
- ⅔ quantity *Meringue* (see recipe p. 18), made into 8 small meringues.
- 1 cup (8 oz/250 g) raspberries
- ⅔ cup (3 oz/90 g) almonds, slivered (flaked) and toasted

MILLEFOGLIE AI LAMPONI
Raspberry mille-feuilles

For best results, prepare the layers of pastry and the filling in advance, but do not make up the dessert until the last moment.

Serves: 6; Preparation: 40 minutes + time to make the puff pastry; Cooking: 45 minutes; Level of difficulty: Complicated

Prepare the pastry. § Prepare the zabaione. § Roll out the pastry very thinly, taking care not to tear it. Cut into four equal squares and prick with a fork. § Place on baking sheets and bake in a preheated oven at 400°F/200°C/gas 6 for 20 minutes. § When golden brown, sprinkle each piece with 1 tablespoon of confectioners' sugar and return to the oven for a few minutes to caramelize. § When the zabaione is completely cold, add the cream and crumbled meringues. § Just before serving, make up the dessert by alternating layers of the pastry, zabaione, raspberries, and almonds. § Sprinkle the top layer with raspberries, almonds, and the remaining confectioners' sugar.

VARIATIONS
– Replace the raspberries with the same quantity of strawberries.
– If short of time, use store-bought puff pastry.

INGREDIENTS

- 2½ cups (20 fl oz/600 ml) heavy (double) cream
- 2–3 drops vanilla extract (essence)
- 4 tablespoons confectioners' (icing) sugar
- 1 quantity *Meringue* (see recipe p. 18), crumbled
- ⅔ cup (5 oz/150 g) marrons glacés, chopped
- rum for the mold

CHOCOLATE SAUCE:
- 5 squares (5 oz/150 g) semi-sweet (dark) chocolate, melted
- 2 tablespoons butter
- ⅓ cup (3½ fl oz/100 ml) light (single) cream

Left: Millefoglie ai lamponi

MATTONELLA MERINGATA
Chestnut ice cream with chocolate sauce

Serves: 6; Preparation: 45 minutes + time to chill; Level of difficulty: Medium

Whip the heavy cream, then add the vanilla extract and the confectioners' sugar. § Fold in the meringues and marrons glacés, taking care not to let the mixture collapse. § Brush an oblong mold with rum. Pour in the mixture and place in the freezer for at least 3 hours. § To make the sauce: melt the chocolate in the top of a double-boiler with the butter and cream, mixing thoroughly with a spatula. § Pour over the ice cream and serve.

VARIATION
– Replace marrons glacés with berry fruit, toasted almonds, chocolate chips, or crushed nut brittle.

Cassata Siciliana
Sicilian Ricotta cake

Serves: 6; Preparation: 2¼ hours; Chilling: 2 hours; Level of difficulty: Complicated

Boil the sugar, water, and vanilla bean in a heavy-bottomed pan until the mixture turns to syrup. Set aside to cool. § Beat the Ricotta vigorously with a spatula, then add the syrup gradually, stirring until the mixture becomes soft and creamy. § Mix the chocolate and candied fruit (reserving some for decoration) with the Ricotta, then add the nuts and Maraschino. § Cut the sponge cake into thin slices and line a springform pan 10 in (25 cm) in diameter with them, adding a little apricot jelly to bind them together. § Fill with the Ricotta mixture, spreading it evenly. § Cover with the remaining sponge and chill in the refrigerator for at least 2 hours. § Prepare the glaze by heating the rest of the apricot jelly, vanilla sugar, and orange flower water, stirring until it becomes syrupy. § Remove the cake from the refrigerator, coat evenly with the glaze and decorate with the reserved pieces of candied fruit.

VARIATION
– This recipe is a simplified one as regards the glaze. The original recipe has fondant icing. To make this, beat 1⅔ cups (8 oz/250 g) confectioners' (icing) sugar with two egg whites. Color with green food coloring and glaze the cake.

■ INGREDIENTS

• 1¼ cups (8 oz/250 g) superfine (caster) sugar
• ½ cup (4 fl oz/125 ml) water
• 1 vanilla bean (pod)
• 2 cups (1 lb/500 g) fresh Ricotta cheese, strained
• 5 squares (5 oz/150 g) semi-sweet (dark) chocolate, chopped in tiny pieces
• 3 cups (12 oz/300 g) mixed candied fruit
• 1½ tablespoons pistachio nuts, shelled
• 2 tablespoons Maraschino or Kirsch liqueur
• 1 quantity *Italian sponge cake* (see recipe p. 14)
• 3 heaped tablespoons apricot jelly (jam)
• 1 tablespoon confectioners' (icing) sugar
• 2 tablespoons orange flower water

Castagnaccio
Chestnut cake
This Tuscan specialty is very easy to prepare.

Serves: 8; Preparation: 20 minutes; Cooking: 1 hour; Level of difficulty: Simple

Place the chestnut flour in a mixing bowl and gradually stir in the water, taking care that no lumps form. § Add the salt and 2½ tablespoons of the pine nuts. § Place the chestnut mixture in a layer about ½ in (1 cm) thick on an oiled baking sheet. Drizzle with the oil and scatter with the rosemary and remaining pine nuts. § Bake in a preheated oven at 400°F/200°/gas 6 for about 1 hour. § Serve immediately.

VARIATION
– Add raisins or chopped walnuts to the mixture.

■ INGREDIENTS

• 4 cups (1 lb/500 g) chestnut flour, sifted
• 3¼ cups (26 fl oz/ 800 ml) cold water
• dash of salt
• 2 tablespoons extra-virgin olive oil
• 1 tablespoon fresh rosemary
• 3 tablespoons pine nuts

Right: *Cassata siciliana*

■ INGREDIENTS

- ⅔ cup (7 oz/200 g) butter, melted
- 8 eggs, separated
- 1 cup (7 oz/200 g) superfine (caster) sugar
- dash of salt
- 2½ cups (8 oz/250 g) all-purpose (plain) flour
- butter and flour for the cake pan
- 3½ cups (14 oz/450 g) mixed berry fruit (wild strawberries, raspberries, blackberries, etc)
- ⅓ cup (2 oz/40 g) confectioners' (icing) sugar

■ INGREDIENTS

- 1⅔ cups (7 oz/200 g) almonds, toasted
- ⅔ cup (3½ oz/100 g) shelled walnuts
- 2 tablespoons candied lemon peel
- 1 cup (7 oz/200 g) candied orange peel
- 1⅓ cups (5 oz/150 g) all-purpose (plain) flour
- ½ teaspoon each, coriander, mace, cloves, nutmeg
- ¾ cup (5 oz/150 g) brown sugar
- ½ cup (5 oz/150 g) honey

SPICE POWDER:

- 3 tablespoons cardamom
- 1 tablespoon cinnamon

Torta ai frutti di bosco
Mixed berry cake

Serves: 6; Preparation: 30 minutes; Cooking: about 1 hour; Level of difficulty: Simple

Cream the butter and sugar, then add the egg yolks one by one. § Beat the egg whites with the salt until stiff and fold them into the mixture. Carefully add the flour and mix well. § Pour the mixture into a buttered and floured springform pan 10 in (25 cm) in diameter. Cover with the berries (some may sink into the batter), reserving a few for decorating. § Bake in a preheated oven at 375°F/190°C/gas 5 for about 1 hour. § Set aside to cool. Sprinkle with the confectioners' sugar and decorate with the reserved berries just before serving.

Panforte
Panforte

A traditional cake from Siena dating from the Middle Ages.

Serves: 8; Preparation: 20 minutes; Cooking: 30 minutes; Level of difficulty: Medium

Chop the almonds and walnuts nuts coarsely. Cut the two candied peels into small diamonds. § Combine the peel in a mixing bowl with the flour and ground spices. § Heat the sugar and honey with 1 tablespoonful of cold water, preferably in a copper pan, and stir until dissolved. § When it starts to form small bubbles on the surface, remove a drop of the syrup with a wooden toothpick and place in cold water. Squeeze the drop between two fingers and if threads form when you open and close them, the syrup is ready. § Remove from heat and add the nut mixture. § Beat well until all the ingredients are well mixed. § Place the mixture on a baking sheet lined with rice paper. Shape the mixture into a disk about ½ in (1 cm) thick. § Sprinkle with the spice powder and bake in a preheated oven at 350°F/150°C/gas 4 for 3 minutes. § Before serving, cut the excess rice paper away from the edges.

Left:
Torta al frutti di bosco

CREAMY DESSERTS

*From chocolate and liqueur-flavored molds
and mousses, to soft puddings and delectable desserts,
this chapter has a host of suggestions for
perfect ways to finish a family
meal or dinner party.*

Tiramisù
Tiramisù

This delicious dessert will never let you down — it is simple to prepare, never goes wrong, and always makes a wonderful impression. Make it the day before and chill in the refrigerator.

Serves: 6; Preparation: 20 minutes; Chilling: at least 3 hours; Level of difficulty: Simple

Whisk the egg yolks and superfine sugar until pale and creamy. § Carefully fold in the Mascarpone. § Beat the egg whites with the salt until very stiff and fold them into the mixture. § Spread a thin layer over the bottom of a large oval serving dish. § Soak the ladyfingers briefly in the coffee and place a layer over the mixture on the bottom of the dish. § Cover with another layer of the mixture and sprinkle with a little chocolate. § Continue in this way until all the ingredients are in the dish. § Finish with a layer of cream and chocolate, and sprinkle with unsweetened cocoa.

VARIATION
– There are many variations. Try using *Zabaione* (see recipe page 20) and crushed praline or nut brittle instead of the Mascarpone mixture.

■ INGREDIENTS

- 5 eggs, separated
- ¾ cup (5 oz/150 g) superfine (caster) sugar
- 2 cups (1 lb/500 g) Mascarpone cheese
- dash of salt
- about 30 ladyfingers (preferably *savoiardi*)
- 1 cup (8 fl oz/250 ml) strong cool coffee
- 7 squares (7 oz/200 g) semi-sweet (dark) chocolate, grated
- 1 tablespoon unsweetened cocoa (cocoa powder)

Bonet
Bonet

This dessert comes from Turin, the capital city of Piedmont and once home to the kings of Italy.

Serves: 6; Preparation: 30 minutes; Cooking: 1 hour; Level of difficulty: Medium

Whisk the eggs and superfine sugar until pale and creamy. § Stir in the unsweetened cocoa and Amaretto di Saronno. § Pour in the milk gradually, stirring constantly, then add the crumbled Amaretti cookies. § Pour the mixture into a buttered pudding mold and place in a roasting pan half-filled with water. § Bake in a preheated oven at 350°F/180°C/gas 4 for about 1 hour. § Cool before unmolding onto a serving dish.

VARIATION
– Sprinkle the buttered mold with crumbled Amaretti cookies to make a delicious crust.

■ INGREDIENTS

- 6 eggs
- 1¼ cup (9 oz/260 g) superfine (caster) sugar
- 2 tablespoons unsweetened cocoa (cocoa powder), sifted
- 2 tablespoons Amaretto di Saronno (almond) liqueur
- 2 cups (16 fl oz/500 ml) milk, very hot
- 6 Amaretti cookies (macaroons), store-bought (or see recipe p. 81), crumbled

Right:
Tiramisù

Crema al croccante di mandorle
Custard with almond brittle

Serves: 4; Preparation: 20 minutes; Cooking: 20 minutes; Level of difficulty: Simple

Bring the lemon zest and milk to a boil. § Place the egg yolks and superfine sugar in a heavy-bottomed saucepan and whisk until pale and creamy. § Mix in the cornstarch and the hot milk and cook the mixture over very low heat until it comes to a boil. § Cook for another 3 minutes, stirring continuously. § Remove from heat and add the almond brittle, reserving some for decoration. § Serve the custard in small individual dishes decorated with the reserved almond brittle.

VARIATION
– Replace the almond brittle with Amaretti cookies (macaroons) and sprinkle the top with unsweetened cocoa.

■ INGREDIENTS

- zest of 1 lemon, in one piece
- 1¼ cups (10 fl oz/300 ml) milk
- 4 egg yolks
- ¾ cup (5 oz/150 g) superfine (caster) sugar
- 4 teaspoons cornstarch (corn flour)
- ⅓ cup (3½ oz/100 g) almond brittle, crushed

Charlotte di mele
Apple charlotte

Charlottes are molded desserts, made in a pan lined with bread, cake, or ladyfingers and filled with fruit, pudding, or cream.

Serves: 8; Preparation: 50 minutes; Cooking: 40 minutes; Level of difficulty: Medium

Chop the apples into bite-sized pieces and cook in a small amount of water until soft and mushy. § Add 3 tablespoons of the superfine sugar and a few drops of vanilla extract and continue cooking until the mixture thickens. § Butter a charlotte mold and line it with baking parchment (paper). § Cut the slices of bread in half and brush with some of the melted butter. Line the mold with them, overlapping slightly. § Beat the egg white with the remaining superfine sugar and brush over the bread. § Finish with a light sprinkling of rum, then pour in the apple purée. § Cover with more bread slices spread with butter and sprinkled with rum. § Bake in a preheated oven at 350°F/180°C/gas 4 for 40 minutes. § Sprinkle with confectioners' sugar and serve.

VARIATION
– Repace the bread with the same weight of ladyfingers soaked in milk and brandy.

■ INGREDIENTS

- 5 cooking apples, peeled and cored
- 4 tablespoons superfine (caster) sugar
- 2–3 drops vanilla extract (essence)
- 10 oz (300 g) sliced white bread, crusts removed
- ¾ cup (7 fl oz/200 ml) butter, melted
- 1 egg white
- 4 tablespoons white rum
- confectioners' (icing) sugar, for sprinkling

Right:
Crema al croccante di mandorle

- 1 quantity *Italian sponge cake* (see recipe p. 14)
- ¾ cup (5 oz/150 g) superfine (caster) sugar
- ¾ cup (7 fl oz/200 ml) water
- 3 tablespoons brandy
- 3 tablespoons rum
- ⅓ cup (1¾ oz/50 g) confectioners' (icing) sugar
- ⅓ cup (3½ oz/100 g) almonds, toasted and ground
- ⅓ cup (3½ oz/100 g) hazelnuts, toasted and ground
- 4 tablespoons candied fruit, chopped
- 5 squares (5 oz/150 g) semi-sweet (dark) chocolate, flaked
- 4 cups (32 fl oz/1 liter) whipped cream

- 2 tablespoons confectioners' (icing) sugar
- 1 cup (8 oz/250 g) raspberries, chopped
- ¼ quantity *Meringue* (see recipe p. 18)
- 2 cups (16 fl oz/500 ml) whipped cream
- 1 cup (8 fl oz/250 ml) raspberry syrup
- 2 tablespoons raspberry liqueur
- 2 tablespoons sugar syrup
- 1 quantity *Italian sponge cake* (see recipe p. 14)
- 20 whole raspberries
- 1 cup (8 fl oz/250 ml) whipped cream

Zuccotto
Skull cap

This Florentine dessert takes its name (the Italian word zuccotto *means "skullcap") from the traditional head coverings worn by church dignitaries.*

Serves: 6-8; Preparation: 40 minutes; Chilling: at least 5 hours; Level of difficulty: Medium

Cut the sponge cake into small slices. § Prepare the syrup by boiling the superfine sugar and water for a few minutes. Remove from heat, add the brandy and rum, and leave to cool. § Moisten the edges of a domed mold with a little syrup and line with half the sliced sponge cake. Brush with the remaining syrup. § Mix the confectioners' sugar, nuts, candied fruit, and chocolate into the whipped cream. Pour the mixture into the dish and cover with the remaining sponge slices. § Chill the dessert for at least 5 hours. § To unmold, dip the dish briefly into cold water.

VARIATION
– Mix 7 squares (7 oz/200 g) of melted semi-sweet chocolate with half the whipped cream to create two layers with two different flavors.

Charlotte al lamponi
Raspberry charlotte

Serves: 6-8 Preparation: 40 minutes; Chilling: overnight; Level of difficulty: Simple

Fold the confectioners' sugar, raspberries, and 1 crumbled meringue into the whipped cream. § Stir in the raspberry syrup (reserving 2 tablespoons) and liqueur. § Cut the sponge into slices and crumble the other meringues. § Brush a charlotte mold with reserved raspberry syrup and line it with slices of sponge cake. § Pour in half the filling and half the crumbled meringues, then add the remaining filling and meringues. § Cover with slices of soaked sponge cake, then chill in the refrigerator overnight. § Unmold the charlotte by placing the mold in warm water for a few minutes. § Serve decorated with raspberries and whipped cream.

VARIATION
– Serve the charlotte with a sauce made by blending ⅓ cup (3½ oz/100 g) raspberries with 4 tablespoons of sugar and a little lemon juice. Place over low heat for a few minutes to thicken, then leave to cool.

Left: *Zuccotto*

Coppa di crema al mascarpone
Chocolate cream

Serves: 6; Preparation: 30 minutes; Chilling: about 2 hours; Level of difficulty: Medium

Beat the egg yolks and superfine sugar until very pale and creamy. Mix in the Mascarpone gently and flavor with Marsala. § Melt the chocolate in the milk over very low heat. Set aside to cool. § Mix the chocolate and milk with one third of the Mascarpone mixture. § Crumble the meringues in the bottom of 6 ice-cream dishes and pour in the Mascarpone and chocolate mixtures. § Blend the surfaces of the two mixtures with a knife to give a marbled effect. § Leave in the refrigerator to chill for at least 2 hours, then serve.

■ INGREDIENTS

- 2 egg yolks
- ½ cup (3 ½ oz/100 g) superfine (caster) sugar
- 1⅓ cups (10 oz/300 g) Mascarpone cheese
- 1 tablespoon Marsala wine
- 4 squares (4 oz/125 g) semi-sweet (dark) chocolate, chopped
- 2 ½ tablespoons milk
- ⅓ quantity *Meringue* (see recipe, p. 18)

ZUPPA INGLESE
Florentine trifle

INGREDIENTS

- ½ cup (4 fl oz/125 ml) Alchermes liqueur
- ½ cup (4 fl oz/125 ml) rum
- about 4 tablespoons water
- 2 tablespoons butter
- about 20 ladyfingers (preferably *savoiardi*)
- 1 quantity *Chocolate pastry cream* (see recipe p. 20)
- 1 quantity *Vanilla pastry cream* (see recipe p. 20)
- 1 cup (8 fl oz/250 ml) whipped cream for decoration

The origins of this dessert date back to the splendid Florentine Renaissance court of the Medici family. Its present name (which translates literally as "English soup") probably dates to the 18th century, when it was apparently a favorite with the large expatriate English community in Florence.

Serves: 6; Preparation: 30 minutes; Chilling: about 12 hours; Level of difficulty: Medium

Mix the Alchermes, rum, and water in an earthenware bowl. § Butter a charlotte mold and line it with ladyfingers dipped in the water and liqueur mixture. § Pour the chocolate cream into the mold, then cover with a layer of dipped ladyfingers and spread the vanilla cream on top. § Finish with the remaining ladyfingers. Cover with foil and chill in the refrigerator for 12 hours. § To unmold, dip the dish briefly in warm water. § Serve decorated with whipped cream.

VARIATIONS
– Replace the ladyfingers with thin slices of Italian sponge cake.
– If Alchermes liqueur is unavailable, use another very sweet liqueur colored red with several drops of cochineal (red food coloring).

COPPA DELIZIA
Cherry delight

INGREDIENTS

- 6 cups (3 lb/1.3 kg) cherries, pitted (stoned)
- ½ cup (3½ oz/100 g) superfine (caster) sugar
- 2–3 drops vanilla extract (essence)
- dash of cinnamon
- 1 quantity *Italian sponge cake* (recipe p. 14)
- 4 tablespoons Maraschino or Kirsch liqueur
- 2 cups (16 fl oz/500 ml) whipped cream

Serves: 6; Preparation: 30 minutes; Chillling: about 1 hour; Level of difficulty: Simple

Place the cherries in a heavy-bottomed saucepan with the sugar, vanilla extract, and cinnamon. § Cook over high heat for about 5 minutes, or until the cherries are lightly caramelized. § Reserve about 20 for decoration. § Slice the sponge thinly and use a part to line a deep serving bowl. Brush with liqueur, then cover with a layer of cherries followed by some whipped cream. Repeat this sequence until all the ingredients are in the bowl. § Decorate the top with the reserved cherries. Chill the dessert in the refrigerator for at least 1 hour before serving.

VARIATION
– Replace the cherries with other kinds of fruit, such as peaches. In this case, use rum instead of Maraschino or Kirsch.

Left:
Coppa di crema al mascarpone

Crème bruciata
Crème brûlée

*Made of baked custard, topped with caramelized sugar,
this dessert is a light yet satisfying way to finish a fairly heavy meal.*

■ INGREDIENTS

• 2 eggs and 7 egg yolks
• 2¼ cups (1 lb/500 g) superfine (caster) sugar
• 2½ cups (16 fl oz/ 500 ml) light (single) cream
• brown sugar for caramelizing

Serves: 6; Preparation: 30 minutes; Cooking: 1 hour; Chilling: 2 hours; Level of difficulty: Simple

Whisk the eggs and egg yolks with the superfine sugar until the mixture falls in ribbons. § Warm the cream slightly and beat it into the mixture. § Pour the mixture into individual ramekin dishes through a strainer. § Arrange the ramekins in a roasting pan lined with baking parchment (paper) to prevent them breaking. Pour water around the ramekins and bake them in a preheated oven at 350°F/180°C/gas 4 for about 1 hour. § Leave to cool then chill in the refrigerator for at least 2 hours. § Just before serving, sprinkle the ramekins with brown sugar and place under a hot broiler (grill) until the sugar is caramelized.

VARIATION
– If preferred, caramelize the brown sugar in a pan on the stove, then pour it over the cold crème brûlée, instead of using the broiler.

Crema al limoncello
Limoncello cream

*Limoncello is a sweet lemon liqueur which is very much in vogue in Italy at the moment. Originally
from the Amalfi coast, near Naples, it is now available throughout the peninsula (and abroad).*

■ INGREDIENTS

• 1 cup (8 fl oz/250 ml) Limoncello liqueur
• *Vanilla pastry cream* made with 4 egg yolks (see recipe p. 20)
• 4 slices candied lemon peel
• 4 tablespoons almonds, slivered (flaked)

Serves: 4; Preparation 15 minutes; Cooking: 10 minutes; Chilling: 1 hour; Level of difficulty: Simple

Prepare the pastry cream. § Stir the Limoncello into the cream and leave to cool with a layer of plastic wrap (clingfilm) over the surface to prevent a skin forming. § Place in individual glass serving dishes and chill for at least 1 hour. § Before serving, decorate with the candied lemon peel and slivered almonds.

VARIATION
– Flavor the cream with other liqueurs, such as Kirsch or Marsala. If using Marsala, serve garnished with ladyfingers and ground pistachio nuts.

Right:
Crema bruciata

- 4 cups (32 fl oz/1 liter) light (single) cream,
- ¾ cup (5 oz/150 g) superfine (caster) sugar
- 2 tablespoons gelatin
- ⅔ cup (5 fl oz/150 ml) strong, hot coffee
- whipped cream to decorate
- coffee beans to decorate

PANNA COTTA AL CAFFÉ
Cooked cream with coffee

Serves: 6; Preparation: 15 minutes; Cooking: 10 minutes; Chilling: about 5 hours; Level of difficulty: Simple

Boil the cream with the superfine sugar. § Dissolve the gelatin in the hot coffee and stir into the cream and sugar. § Pour the mixture into a domed or rectangular mold, and when it begins to set (not before, otherwise the gelatin and cream will separate) refrigerate for at least 5 hours. § Serve decorated with whipped cream and coffee beans.

Babà al rhum
Rum baba

The word "baba" is of Polish origin, and so, it seems, is this dessert. But in Italy, the baba is just one more exquisite Neapolitan treat. There are many different versions of the rum baba. This is a home recipe, easy to make, and guaranteed to be successful.

Serves: 6; Preparation: 20 minutes; Cooking: 15 minutes; Level of difficulty: Medium

Dissolve the yeast in a little warm water and set aside until it foams. § Beat the eggs and superfine sugar until pale and creamy. § Gradually add the oil, butter, and yeast mixture. § Lastly, stir in the sifted flour and salt. § Knead the mixture vigorously, until it forms a soft, elastic dough. § Fill baba molds just under half full, then cover and leave in a warm place to let the dough rise. § When the dough has risen to just below the rim of each mold, bake in a preheated oven at 350°F/180°C/gas 4 for about 15 minutes. § Meanwhile, prepare the rum syrup by boiling the superfine sugar and water for about 10 minutes, until the mixture is syrupy. § Add the lemon and rum and leave to cool. § When the babas are cooked, leave to cool for a while, then soak in the rum syrup and leave on a wire rack to drain.

> VARIATIONS
> – In Naples, babas are often served with whipped cream.
> – Some recipes suggest glazing the babas with apricot jelly (jam) dissolved in a little warm water.

■ INGREDIENTS

- 1 oz (30 g) fresh yeast or 2 packages active dry yeast
- 4 tablespoons lukewarm water
- 5 eggs
- 2 tablespoons superfine (caster) sugar
- ½ cup (4 fl oz/125 ml) extra-virgin olive oil
- 4 tablespoons butter, melted and cooled,
- 3 cups (12 oz/350 g) all-purpose (plain) flour
- dash of salt

RUM SYRUP:
- 1⅓ cup (10 oz/300 g) superfine (caster) sugar
- 2 cups (16 fl oz/500 ml) water
- 1 lemon, sliced
- ½ cup (4 fl oz/125 ml) rum

Dolceriso
Dolceriso

Serves: 6; Preparation: 1 hour; Cooking: 1 hour; Level of difficulty: Simple

Bring the milk to a boil. Add half the brown sugar and the salt and cook until the sugar has dissolved. Add the rice and continue to cook until all the milk has been absorbed. § Remove from heat, stir in the butter and leave to cool. § To make the filling, peel 3 of the pears. Dice them finely and cook with the lemon juice and all but 1 tablespoon of the remaining brown sugar until soft and syrupy. § Now add the eggs to the rice, one at a time. § Pour half the rice mixture into a springform pan 8 in (20 cm) in diameter, and sprinkle with the bread crumbs. § Cover with two-thirds of the pear mixture, then add another layer of rice, followed by the remaining pears. § Peel the reserved pear. Slice it thinly and arrange over the top. § Sprinkle with the remaining brown sugar and bake in a preheated oven at 350°F/180°C/gas 4 for about 1 hour.

■ INGREDIENTS

- 4 cups (32 fl oz/1 liter) milk
- 1 cup (3½ oz/100 g) brown sugar
- dash of salt
- 1¼ cups (8 oz/250 g) short-grain rice (preferably arborio)
- 4 tablespoons butter
- 4 pears
- juice of ½ lemon
- 2 whole eggs and 2 yolks
- 4 tablespoons dry bread crumbs

Right:
Babà al rhum

MONTE BIANCO
Mont Blanc

- 1 lb (500 g) chestnuts, shelled
- dash of salt
- 1 bay leaf
- ½ cup (2 oz/60 g) unsweetened cocoa (cocoa powder)
- 1¼ cups (6 oz/180 g) confectioners' (icing) sugar
- 2 tablespoons white rum
- 1¼ cups (10 fl oz/300 ml) whipped cream

Serves: 4-6; Preparation: 40 minutes; Cooking: 40 minutes; Chilling: 1 hour; Level of difficulty: Medium

Cover the chestnuts with water, then add the salt and bay leaf and bring to a boil. § Cook for about 40 minutes, then peel the chestnuts, removing the inner skin. Mash them with a potato-masher while still hot, then place in a mixing bowl and stir in the unsweetened cocoa, confectioners' sugar, and rum. § Put the purée through a potato-ricer or strainer, letting it drop onto the serving dish in a little mound of vermicelli. § Chill for at least 1 hour. § Cover with whipped cream just before serving.

VARIATION
– Decorate the dessert with marrons glacés and candied violets.

MOUSSE DI RICOTTA CON SALSA DI PRUGNE
Ricotta mousse with plum sauce

The acidity of plums is a good counterbalance to the blandness of cream cheese in desserts.

- 1½ cups (12 oz/350 g) Ricotta cheese
- ⅓ cup (3 oz/90 g) vanilla sugar
- 3 egg yolks
- grated zest of 1 lemon
- 1 tablespoon rum
- ⅔ cup (5 fl oz/150 ml) whipped cream
- 2 squares (2 oz/60 g) semi-sweet (dark) chocolate, plus more for decoration
- 2 tablespoons candied orange peel, chopped
- 1 lb (500 g) plums, pitted (stoned)
- ½ cup (3½ oz/100 g) brown sugar
- juice of ½ lemon

Serves: 6; Preparation: 20 minutes; Cooking: 15 minutes; Chilling: 1 hour; Level of difficulty: Simple

Cream the Ricotta and vanilla sugar. § Add the yolks, lemon zest, and rum and beat until smooth. § Pour the mixture into a large mixing bowl and carefully fold in the cream, chocolate, and peel (reserve a few pieces for decoration). Chill in the refrigerator for at least 1 hour. § Meanwhile, cook the plums, brown sugar, and lemon juice over high heat until the mixture thickens and then whisk it until reduced to a sauce. § Place the mousse in individual bowls for serving, then pour the hot plum sauce over the top. Decorate with flaked chocolate and candied orange peel.

Left:
Mousse di ricotta con salsa di prugne

VARIATION
– If fresh plums are not available, use jelly (jam) heated with a few tablespoons of water.

Mousse di mascarpone con fragole
Mascarpone mousse with strawberries

Serves: 4; Preparation: 30 minutes; Chilling: 4 hours; Level of difficulty: Simple

Dissolve the gelatin in a little hot water, then add half to the liqueur and the other half to the wine. Stir both mixtures well, then set them aside to cool. § Beat the egg whites with the salt until stiff, then carefully fold in the confectioners' sugar. § Mix the Mascarpone with the jellied liqueur, then fold in the cream and lastly the egg white mixture. § Chill the mousse for about 4 hours. § Slice the strawberries thinly and place them in individual serving dishes. Pour over a little of the jellied wine and fill the dishes with the mousse. Sprinkle with confectioners' sugar and serve the rest of the jellied wine separately.

VARIATION
– Replace the strawberries with an equal quantity of raspberries.

■ INGREDIENTS

- 2 tablespoons gelatin
- 4 tablespoons strawberry liqueur
- 1¼ cups (10 fl oz/300 ml) fruity white wine
- 2 egg whites
- dash of salt
- ½ cup (2¾ oz /50 g) confectioners' (icing) sugar, plus extra for sprinkling
- 1 cup (8 oz/250 g) Mascarpone cheese
- ¾ cup (7 fl oz/200 ml) heavy (double) cream, whipped
- 1 cup (8 oz/250 g) strawberries

Mousse di castagne al cioccolato
Chestnut mousse with chocolate

Serves: 6; Preparation: 20 minutes + 2 hours to chill; Level of difficulty: Simple

Place the chestnut purée (made by mashing boiled chestnuts; see recipe for Mont Blanc on page 73) in a mixing bowl . § Melt the chocolate in the top of a double-boiler and then add it to the purée with the cream. Mix thoroughly. § Beat the egg whites with the salt until stiff, then add the confectioners' sugar and mix carefully until the mixture becomes glossy. § Add the chestnut purée and use a spatula to mix the ingredients thoroughly. § Chill the mousse in the refrigerator for at least 2 hours. Serve in individual dishes, decorated with marrons glacés and sprinkled with chocolate shavings.

VARIATION
– Served with a bowl of stiffly whipped cream.

■ INGREDIENTS

- 1 cup (8 oz/250 g) chestnut purée
- 3½ squares (3½ oz/100 g) semi-sweet (dark) chocolate
- ¾ cup (7 fl oz/200 ml) light (single) cream
- 2 egg whites
- dash of salt
- ½ cup (3 oz/90 g) confectioners' (icing) sugar
- 6 marrons glacés to decorate
- semi-sweet (dark) chocolate shavings for sprinkling

Right:
Mousse di castagne al cioccolato

INGREDIENTS

- 12 squares (12 oz/350 g) semi-sweet (dark) chocolate
- 6 eggs, separated
- 4 tablespoons confectioners' (icing) sugar
- ¾ cup (7 fl oz/200 ml) light (single) cream

Mousse al cioccolato
Chocolate mousse

Serves: 8; Preparation: 30 minutes; Chilling: about 12 hours; Level of difficulty: Simple

Melt the chocolate in the top of a double-boiler and leave until tepid. § Whisk the egg yolks and confectioners' sugar until very pale and creamy. Add the melted chocolate and return to heat for a few minutes, stirring all the time. Set aside to cool. § Whip the cream and the egg whites separately. § Carefully fold the egg whites and cream into the cooled egg-and-chocolate mixture, taking great care not to let the mixture collapse. § Chill the mousse for about 12 hours before serving.

Budino di riso dell'Artusi
Rice pudding Artusi-style

Food writer Pellegrino Artusi published L'Arte di mangiar bene *(The Art of Eating Well) back in 1891, yet it remains the best-selling cook book in Italy. Artusi, who chose and classified 790 home recipes from Tuscany and Emilia Romagna, was the first Italian food writer to write about everyday recipes and cooking. This is one of his classic desserts.*

Serves: 8; Preparation: 15 minutes; Cooking: 35 minutes; Level of difficulty: Simple

Place the rice, milk, and vanilla bean over medium heat. Bring to a boil, add the superfine sugar, raisins, peel, salt, and butter, and simmer for 10 minutes. § When cooked, remove from heat. Remove the vanilla bean and set the mixture aside to cool. § Add the eggs one at a time, and then the rum. Pour this mixture into a buttered pudding basin coated with the bread crumbs. § Bake in a preheated oven at 350°F/180°C/gas 4 for about 35 minutes. Unmold and serve while still warm.

VARIATION
– Serve with 1 quantity *Vanilla pastry cream* (see recipe page 20).

■ INGREDIENTS

- 1 cup (5 oz/150 g) short-grain rice (preferably arborio)
- 4 cups (32 fl oz/1 liter) milk
- 1 vanilla bean (pod)
- ⅓ cup (3 oz/90 g) superfine (caster) sugar
- ½ cup (3½ oz/100 g) golden raisins (sultanas),
- 1½ tablespoons mixed candied peel, chopped
- dash of salt
- 1 tablespoon butter
- 2 whole eggs and 2 yolks
- 1 cup (8 fl oz/250 ml) rum or Cognac
- 2 tablespoons butter for greasing the pudding basin
- 4 tablespoons bread crumbs

Soffiato di pesche
Peach soufflé

Serves: 4; Preparation: 15 minutes; Cooking: about 1 hour; Level of difficulty: Simple

Cream the butter, superfine sugar, and salt together. § Add the egg yolks one by one, then the Ricotta. Mix in the cornstarch, lemon juice and zest, and almonds. § Beat the egg whites until stiff, and fold gently into the mixture. Add the peaches and pour the mixture into 4 timbale molds coated with bread crumbs. § Bake in a preheated oven at 325°F/160°C/gas 3 for about 1 hour. Serve warm, sprinkled with confectioners' sugar.

VARIATION
– Try this recipe with other kinds of fruit, such as apricots or nectarines.

■ INGREDIENTS

- 3½ tablespoons butter
- ½ cup (3½ oz/100 g) superfine (caster) sugar
- dash of salt
- 2 eggs, separated
- 1 cup (8 oz/250 g) Ricotta cheese, strained
- ⅓ cup (1¼ oz/40 g) cornstarch (corn flour),
- zest and juice of 1 lemon,
- 2 tablespoons almonds, toasted and ground
- 3 large yellow peaches, pitted (stoned) and sliced
- 4 tablespoons bread crumbs
- 2 tablespoons confectioners' (icing) sugar

Right: Budino di riso dell'Artusi

Cookies

Every Italian region has its own special cookies.
There are many variations on the classic recipes.
In this chapter I have included our family favorites.

INGREDIENTS

- 3 cups (14 oz/450 g) almonds, toasted
- 1½ cups (12 oz/350 g) superfine (caster) sugar
- 5 egg whites
- dash of cinnamon

BRUTTI MA BUONI
Ugly but good

These cookies owe their name to the fact that they do not actually look particularly inviting. But their crispness and delicious almond flavor make them the perfect snack, or after-dinner treat, accompanied by dessert wine or coffee.

Serves: 6-8; Preparation: 40 minutes; Cooking: 30 minutes; Level of difficulty: Medium

Finely chop the almonds with 2 tablespoons of the sugar in a food processor. § Beat the egg whites until stiff and fold in the remaining sugar, almonds, and cinnamon. § Cook this mixture over very low heat, stirring continuously, until it comes away from the sides of the saucepan. Set aside for a few minutes. § Place heaped teaspoonfuls of the mixture on a baking sheet lined with baking parchment (paper). Allow room for spreading. § Bake in a preheated oven at 300°F/150°C/gas 2 for 30 minutes. § Serve cold.

VARIATION
– Try adding 2 tablespoons of unsweetened cocoa (cocoa powder) to the mixture. They are also delicious with toasted hazelnuts instead of almonds.

INGREDIENTS

- 1½ cups (6 oz/180 g) sweet almonds, toasted
- 3 teaspoons bitter almonds, toasted
- 2½ cups (10 oz/300 g) confectioners' (icing) sugar
- 2 egg whites

AMARETTI
Macaroons

Bitter almonds are an indispensable ingredient in these tasty cookies. Indeed, they owe their name to them ("amaro" meaning "bitter"). There are many recipes, but the one I have chosen is a classic version and sure to be a success. If you cannot get bitter almonds, add a few drops of almond extract (essence) to sweet almonds.

Makes: about 30; Preparation: 20 minutes; Cooking: 30 minutes; Level of difficulty: Medium

Finely chop the sweet and bitter almonds with a little confectioners' sugar in a food processor. § Place in a mixing bowl and add half the confectioners' sugar, then one of the egg whites, followed by the remaining sugar, and the second egg white. § Mix by hand until smooth. Roll into cylinders 1–2 in (2.5–5 cm) in diameter. Cut into slices about ½ in (1 cm) thick, then form into balls, and squash them slightly. § Place on a buttered and floured baking sheet. Allow room for spreading. Sprinkle with confectioners' sugar, then bake in a preheated oven at 450°F/230°C/gas 7 for 30 minutes. Serve cold.

Left:
Brutti ma buoni and Amaretti

Ricciarelli
Ricciarelli

These traditional cookies from Siena are thought to be of Arab origin, imported during the Crusades.

Serves: 4; Preparation: 1 hour, + 5-6 hours to rest the dough; Cooking: 15 minutes; Level of difficulty: Complicated

Finely chop the sweet and bitter almonds (or extract) with the flour, ammonium bicarbonate, and orange peel in a food processor. § Put the superfine sugar and water in a saucepan and cook over a low heat until the mixture forms a thin syrup. Add to the almond paste and set aside for 5–6 hours. § Beat the egg white with the confectioners' sugar until stiff and then work it into the dough. § Sprinkle a work surface with flour. Roll the dough out to about ½ in (1 cm) thick. Cut into diamonds measuring about 2 in (5 cm) long. § Place on a baking sheet lined with rice paper, allowing room for spreading. Bake in a preheated oven at 300°F/150°C/gas 2 for about 15 minutes. They should not be brown, so take care not to overbake. § Sprinkle with confectioners' sugar and serve.

■ INGREDIENTS
- 2 cups (8 oz/250 g) sweet almonds, toasted and ground
- 3 teaspoons bitter almonds, ground, or 3 drops almond extract (essence)
- 2 tablespoons all-purpose (plain) flour, plus some extra for the work surface
- dash of ammonium bicarbonate (hartshorn)
- 3 teaspoons candied orange peel, chopped
- ⅔ cup (4 oz/125 g) superfine (caster) sugar
- 3 tablespoons water
- 1 egg white
- 2 teaspoons confectioners' (icing) sugar, plus some extra to sprinkle on the cookies

Biscottini di Prato
Prato cookies

In Tuscany these are an almost obligatory ending to a meal.
They are dipped in Vin Santo while lingering at the table.

Makes: about 2 lb (1 kg) of cookies; Preparation: 30 minutes; Cooking: 30 minutes; Level of difficulty: Medium

Mix the orange zest with the sifted flour and baking powder. Place on a work surface, make a well in the center, and fill with the superfine sugar, eggs, and salt. § Work the ingredients together briefly, then add the almonds, a few at a time. Knead the mixture vigorously, until it forms a soft, elastic dough. § Shape into cylinders about 1 in (2.5 cm) in diameter. Arrange on a buttered and floured baking sheet and brush with egg white. § Bake in a preheated oven at 325°F/160°C/gas 3 for about 15 minutes. § Slice the cylinders diagonally into pieces about 1 in (2.5 cm) long and return to the oven for 15 minutes, or until golden brown. § Serve when cold.

■ INGREDIENTS
- grated zest of 1 orange
- 4 cups (1 lb/500 g) all-purpose (plain) flour
- 1 teaspoon baking powder
- 1 cup (7 oz/200 g) superfine (caster) sugar
- 2 whole eggs, 2 yolks, and 2 egg whites
- dash of salt
- 1¾ cups (8 oz/250 g) almonds, whole

VARIATION
– Add a dash of saffron to the dough for extra color.

Right:
Ricciarelli and Biscottini di Prato

CRESTINE ALLA CREMA
Cream crescents

■ INGREDIENTS

- 1 quantity *Vanilla pastry cream* (see recipe p. 20)
- 2 cups (1 lb/500 g) all-purpose (plain) flour
- 1 cup (7 oz/200 g) superfine (caster) sugar
- 1 tablespoon vanilla sugar
- 1 cup (8 oz/250 g) butter, softened
- grated zest of 1 lemon
- 2 egg yolks
- dash of salt
- 3 teaspoons baking powder
- 2 tablespoons vanilla sugar for sprinkling

Serves: 6; Preparation: 30 minutes; Cooking: 20 minutes; Level of difficulty: Medium

Prepare the vanilla pastry cream and leave to cool. § Sift the flour onto a clean work surface, shape into a mound, and make a well in the center. Add the first measures of superfine and vanilla sugars, as well as the butter, lemon zest, egg yolks, and salt. § Work the ingredients together quickly, adding the baking powder last. § Roll the dough out to a thickness of ¼ in (6 mm) and use a cookie (pastry) cutter, or large glass, to cut out rounds. § Place a tablespoonful of the pastry cream on one side of each round, and fold the pastry in half to form a crescent-shaped cookies. Press down on the edges to seal the cream in. Continue until all the dough and cream are used up. § Place the cookies on a buttered and floured baking sheet, allowing room for spreading. Bake in a preheated oven at 350°F/180°C/gas 4 for about 20 minutes. Sprinkle with the remaining vanilla sugar and serve.

VARIATION
— You can also fill these crescents with thick jelly (jam) or fruit purée.

DELIZIE ALL'UVA
Grape delights

■ INGREDIENTS

- 15 large white seedless grapes
- 2 tablespoons rum
- ½ cup (4 fl oz/125 ml) water
- 1¼ cups (8 oz/250 g) superfine (caster) sugar
- 6 rusks (Zwieback)
- 2¼ cups (8 oz/250 g) almonds, ground
- 1 cup (3½ oz/100 g) unsweetened cocoa (cocoa powder)

These candies do not keep for long, so try and eat them all straight away.

Serves: 6; Preparation: 20 minutes + time to settle; Cooking: 5 minutes; Level of difficulty: Simple

Toss the grapes in 1 tablespoonful of rum. § Heat the water and superfine sugar in a pan and stir until the sugar is completely dissolved. § Crumble the rusks to powder and sprinkle with the remaining rum, then stir the mixture into the sugar mixture, together with the almonds and 1 tablespoonful of unsweetened cocoa. § When cool, take a small piece of the mixture and place a grape in the center, then form into a small ball. Roll in the unsweetened cocoa and set aside. Coat all the grapes in this way and leave for a few hours before serving.

Right:
Crestine alla crema

Tartufi al Cioccolato
Chocolate truffles

Quick and easy to make, these little homemade chocolates are perfect with coffee.

Serves: 6; Preparation: 30 minutes; Chilling: 2 hours; Level of difficulty: Simple

Cream the butter and confectioners' sugar, then beat in the egg yolks one at a time. § Bring the cream to the boil, then add the vanilla sugar and stir to dissolve. Pour the hot cream into the butter mixture and stir in the chocolate. Chill for at least 2 hours. § Using a tablespoon, form into balls and roll in the unsweetened cocoa. § Store in the refrigerator until it is time to serve.

> VARIATION
> – Roll the balls in granulated sugar or flavor the cream with a liqueur of your choice.

■ INGREDIENTS

- 3½ tablespoons butter
- ⅓ cup (1¾ oz/50 g) confectioners' (icing) sugar
- 2 egg yolks
- ⅓ cup (3½ fl oz/100 ml) light (single) cream
- 2 tablespoons vanilla sugar
- 12 squares (12 oz/350 g) semi-sweet (dark) chocolate, grated
- 4 tablespoons unsweetened cocoa (cocoa powder)

Cioccolatini Pralinati
Chocolate pralines

Serves: 5; Preparation: 1 hour; Chilling: 2 hours; Cooking: 20 minutes; Level of difficulty: Complicated

Melt the chocolate in the top of a double-boiler. Stir in the coffee, butter, and 4 tablespoons of the superfine sugar and leave to cool. § When lukewarm, stir in the egg yolks. Place this mixture in the refrigerator until solid. § Heat the remaining superfine sugar in the water and when the sugar is dissolved, add the hazelnuts. Continue to stir over low heat until the mixture darkens. § Spread out on an oiled work surface, and leave to cool. Chop this praline mixture finely in a blender. § Shape the solid chocolate mixture into a roll. § Lightly whisk the egg whites. Dip the roll into them and then into the praline, making sure that the coating sticks. Chill for 2 hours. § Just before serving, cut into slices to make individual chocolates.

■ INGREDIENTS

- 8 squares (8 oz/250 g) semi-sweet (dark) chocolate
- 1 tablespoon strong hot coffee
- 4 tablespoons butter
- 1 cup (7 oz/200 g) superfine (caster) sugar
- 1½ cups (6 oz/180 g) hazelnuts, ground
- 2 eggs, separated
- ⅓ cup (3½ fl oz/100 ml) water
- oil for the work surface

> VARIATION
> – Roll the chocolates in grated coconut instead of the praline.

Right:
Cioccolatini pralinati and
Tartufi al cioccolato

- 1⅓ cups (10 oz/300 g) brown sugar
- ⅔ cup (4 oz/125 g) granulated sugar
- 1 cup (7 fl oz/200 ml) light (single) cream
- ¾ cup (4 fl oz/125 ml) milk
- 1⅓ cups (5 oz/150 g) almonds, ground
- 10 drops vanilla extract (essence)

CROCCANTINI
Croccantini

Makes about 20; Preparation: 15 minutes; Cooking: 15 minutes; Level of difficulty: Simple

Combine the 2 sugars with the cream and milk over medium heat and bring to a boil, then beat with an electric whisk until creamy. § Stir in the almonds and vanilla extract, then divide the mixture into small balls. § Place on a baking sheet lined with baking parchment (paper). Bake in a preheated oven at 350°F/180°C/gas 4 for about 15 minutes, or until golden brown. Serve cold.

Fritters and Crêpes

Many of the best regional sweets and treats in Italy are quickly fried in olive oil, sprinkled with superfine or confectioners' sugar, and served piping hot.

Tortelli dolci di ricotta
Sweet tortelli with Ricotta cheese

For crisp, light, golden brown fritters, fry them in small batches. The temperature of the oil should always be high so that the batter doesn't soak it up.

Serves: 6; Preparation: 15 minutes + time for the dough to rest; Cooking: 20 minutes; Level of difficulty: Simple

Strain the Ricotta and place in a mixing bowl. § Add the eggs, superfine sugar, orange zest, salt, baking soda, and soaked raisins. Lastly, stir in the sifted flour. Work the mixture into a smooth, well-mixed dough and leave to rest for about 1 hour. § Heat the oil to very hot in a large skillet (frying pan) and fry spoonfuls of the mixture until golden brown. Drain on paper towels. Roll them in the confectioners' sugar and serve hot.

■ INGREDIENTS

- 1½ cups (12 oz/350 g) Ricotta cheese
- 3 eggs
- ⅓ cup (3 oz/90 g) superfine (caster) sugar
- grated zest of 1 orange
- dash of salt
- dash of baking soda (bicarbonate of soda)
- 4 tablespoons raisins, soaked in rum overnight
- 1½ cups (6 oz/180 g) all-purpose (plain) flour
- 2 cups (16 fl oz/500 ml) oil, for frying
- 1 cup (5 oz/150 g) confectioners' (icing) sugar

Sfrappole
Carnival fritters

With minor variations, these fritters are made in all regions of Italy at Carnival time, the period leading up to Lent. They are known under under different names depending on the region. This recipe has come down through my husband's family, who originally came from Emilia-Romagna.

Serves: 8-10; Preparation: 20 minutes + time to rest; Cooking: 15 minutes; Level of difficulty: Simple

Sift the flour onto a clean work surface, add the superfine sugar and salt, and shape into a mound. Make a well in the center and break the eggs into it, then add the softened butter and cognac. Mix the ingredients together carefully and leave the dough to rest in a warm place for 2–3 hours. § Roll out a sheet of dough ⅛ in (3 mm) thick and cut it into strips about 1 in (2.5 cm) wide, using a ravioli wheel or knife. § Make the Sfrappole by tying a knot in each strip. Heat the oil to very hot in a large skillet (frying pan) and fry in small batches until light golden brown. § Sprinkle with confectioners' sugar while still hot.

■ INGREDIENTS

- 4 cups (1 lb/500 g) all-purpose (plain) flour
- 2 tablespoons superfine (caster) sugar
- dash of salt
- 4 eggs
- 2 tablespoons butter
- ½ cup (4 fl oz/125 ml) cognac
- 2 cups (16 fl oz/500 ml) oil, for frying
- confectioners' (icing) sugar for sprinkling

VARIATION
– The original recipe uses lard for frying. This gives the Sfrappole more flavor, but they will also be heavier. You can also use white wine instead of cognac.

Right:
Sfrappole

INGREDIENTS

- 2½ cups (1 lb/500 g) short-grain rice (preferably arborio)
- 2 cups (16 fl oz/500 ml) water
- 4 cups (32 fl oz/1 liter) milk
- 1 cup (8 oz/250 g) superfine (caster) sugar
- grated zest of 1 lemon
- dash of salt
- 3 egg yolks
- 2 tablespoons all-purpose (plain) flour
- 2–3 drops vanilla extract (essence)
- 1½ quarts (3 pints/1½ liters) oil for frying
- a little confectioners' sugar to sprinkle on the fritters

INGREDIENTS

- 4 cups (1 lb/500 g) all-purpose (plain) flour,
- 1 cup (7 oz/200 g) superfine (caster) sugar
- 1 tablespoon baking powder
- 3 eggs
- 4 tablespoons butter, melted
- 3 tablespoons Sassolino liqueur (or dark rum)
- 1½ cups (14 oz/450 g) black cherry jelly (jam)
- 2 cups (16 fl oz/500 ml) oil, for frying
- confectioners' (icing) sugar

FRITTELLE DI SAN GIUSEPPE
St. Joseph's fritters

Rice fritters are popular in more or less all parts of northern Italy. They are given this name in Tuscany because they are usually made on St. Joseph's Day — March 19.

Makes: 50 fritters; Preparation: 20 minutes + time to rest; Cooking: 1 hour; Level of difficulty: Medium

Boil the rice in the water and milk, together with the superfine sugar and lemon zest (yellow part only) and salt until all the liquid is absorbed. Leave to settle overnight. § The next day, stir in the egg yolks one at a time, then add the flour and vanilla extract. § Form the mixture into roughly-shaped balls with aid of a teaspoon, taking care not to make them too small. Heat the oil to very hot in a large skillet (frying pan) and fry the fritters until golden brown. Drain on paper towels. § When cold, roll in the confectioners' sugar and serve.

VARIATION
– Flavor the dough with liqueur or add grated orange zest.

RAVIOLINI DI MARMELLATA
Jelly-filled fritters

A typical dish from Emilia-Romagna, traditionally eaten at Carnival time.

Preparation 1 hour + time for the dough to rest; Cooking: 30 minutes; Level of difficulty: Medium

Mix the sifted flour with the superfine sugar and baking powder. Pour the mixture onto a work surface and make a well in the center. § Break the eggs into the well, add the melted butter a little at a time and the liqueur. Work the ingredients together until the dough is smooth and elastic, then leave to rest for at least 1 hour. § Roll the dough out to a thickness of ¼ in (6 mm) and cut out 2-in (5-cm) disks using a round cookie cutter. Place a little jelly on one half of each disk, then fold the other half over and seal the edges. § Heat the oil to very hot in a large skillet (frying pan) and fry the fritters a few at a time until golden brown. Drain on paper towels. § Serve hot, sprinkled with confectioners' sugar.

VARIATION
– You can use whatever jelly (jam) you like as long as the consistency is firm. In the traditional recipe, the Raviolini are fried in lard.

Left:

Frittelle di San Giuseppe

CREMA FRITTA ALLA CANNELLA
Fried cinnamon custard

This recipes comes from traditional Venetian and Lombard cooking.

Serves: 4; Preparation: 30 minutes + time for the custard to cool; Cooking: 20 minutes; Level of difficulty: Simple

Prepare a thick pastry cream following the instructions on page 20, but first boiling the milk together with the cinnamon stick. Leave the pastry cream to cool slightly. § Pour onto an oil-coated work surface and spread out to a thickness of 1 in (2.5 cm). When completely cold and firm, cut out shapes with a cookie cutter. Dip in the egg whites and coat with bread crumbs. Heat the oil to very hot in a large skillet (frying pan) and fry a few at a time until golden brown. Drain on paper towels and serve.

VARIATION
– Make a thick *Vanilla pastry cream* (see recipe page 20) and fry as above.

■ INGREDIENTS

- 1 quantity *Lemon pastry cream* (see recipe p. 20)
- 1 stick cinnamon
- 2 egg whites, lightly beaten
- ¾ cup (3½ oz/100 g) dry bread crumbs
- 2 cups (16 fl oz/500 ml) oil, for frying

CANNOLI ALLA SICILIANA
Sicilian-style fritters with Ricotta cheese

The basic ingredient in this well-known dessert is Ricotta cheese.
It should be made from ewe's milk and be extremely fresh.

Serves: 8-10; Preparation: 1 hour + time for the dough to rest; Cooking: 30 minutes; Level of difficulty: Complicated

Sift the flour onto a clean work surface, add the superfine sugar, salt, and unsweetened cocoa, and shape into a mound. Make a well in the center and break the egg into it. Add the softened butter, coffee, and lemon juice and zest. Mix well together, using as much wine as necessary to form a smooth, elastic dough. Leave to rest for 3 hours. § Roll the dough out into a thin sheet and cut into 4-in (10-cm) squares. Wrap each square round a Cannoli tube, sealing two opposite corners together. § Heat the oil to very hot in a large skillet (frying pan) and fry the cannoli until light golden brown. Drain and cool on paper towels, then remove them from the Cannoli tubes. § Strain the Ricotta, then add the superfine sugar, candied lemon peel, chocolate chips, and lemon zest. § Just before serving, fill the Cannoli with the Ricotta mixture, using a pastry (piping) bag, and sprinkle with confectioners' sugar.

■ INGREDIENTS

FOR THE PASTRY:
- 4 cups (1 lb/500 g) all-purpose (plain) flour
- 3 tablespoons superfine (caster) sugar
- dash of salt
- 2 teaspoons unsweetened cocoa (cocoa powder)
- 1 egg
- 3 tablespoons butter
- 2 tablespoons strong cool coffee
- sweet white wine, as required
- 2 cups (16 fl oz/500 ml) oil, for frying

FILLING:
- 2 cups (1 lb/500 g) ewe's milk Ricotta cheese
- 1⅓ cups (10 oz/300 g) superfine (caster) sugar
- 2 cups (7 oz/200 g) candied lemon peel
- 2 cups (7 oz/200 g) chocolate chips
- grated zest of 1 lemon
- confectioners' (icing) sugar

Right: Cannoli alla siciliana

Frittelle di mele con gelato di vaniglia
Apple fritters with vanilla ice cream

Serves: 8; Preparation: 20 minutes + 1 hour for the batter to rest; Cooking: 20 minutes; Level of difficulty: Medium

Prepare the batter by beating the flour with the egg yolks, oil, grappa, and a dash of salt, then adding the water slowly, stirring all the time, until the mixture is smooth but not too liquid. Chill in the refrigerator for at least 1 hour. § Meanwhile, peel and core the apples. Cut them into rings approximately ½ in (1 cm) thick and sprinkle with lemon juice to prevent the flesh from browning. § Beat the egg whites with a dash of salt. Remove the batter from the refrigerator and gently fold in the egg whites. Dip the slices of apple in the batter. § Heat the oil to very hot in a large skillet (frying pan) and fry the apples a few at a time until golden brown. § Drain on paper towels, then sprinkle with confectioners' sugar. § Serve in individual dishes with a scoop of vanilla ice cream.

> Variation
> – Replace the water with the same quantity of milk.
> – Sprinkle the fritters with brown sugar or moisten with honey.

■ INGREDIENTS

- 2 cups (7 oz/200 g) all-purpose (plain) flour
- 2 eggs, separated
- 2 tablespoons oil
- 2 tablespoons grappa
- 2 dashes salt
- about 1 cup (8 fl oz/ 250 ml) water
- 3 russet apples
- 4 tablespoons lemon juice
- 2 cups (16 fl oz/500 ml) oil, for frying
- confectioners' (icing) sugar, for sprinkling
- 1⅓ cups (10 oz/300 g) vanilla ice cream

Struffoli
Christmas fritters

This dessert is popular all over southern Italy, where it is often served at Christmas.

Serves: 10; Preparation: 1 hour; Cooking: 30 minutes; Level of difficulty: Medium

Pour the sifted flour onto a clean work surface and make a well in the center. Place the eggs, superfine sugar, liqueur, and salt in the well and work the ingredients together until they form a smooth elastic dough. § Leave to rest for a while, then divide into pieces and shape them by hand into sticks the thickness of a pencil. Cut each stick into sections no wider than ½ in (1 cm). § Heat the oil to very hot in a large skillet (frying pan) and fry a few at a time. Drain on paper towels. § Heat the honey until thoroughly melted. Add the Struffoli, and candied orange and lemon peels, and stir well to ensure that the honey is distributed evenly. § Tip the Struffoli out onto a serving dish and shape into a mound. Decorate with the sprinkles and serve.

■ INGREDIENTS

- 4 cups (1 lb/500 g) all-purpose (plain) flour
- 4 eggs
- 2 tablespoons superfine (caster) sugar
- ½ cup (4 fl oz/125 ml) liqueur (Strega or anise)
- dash of salt
- 2 cups (16 fl oz/500 ml) oil, for frying
- ⅔ cup (8 oz/250 g) honey
- ¾ cup (3 oz/90 g) each candied orange and lemon peel, diced
- 2 tablespoons sprinkles (hundreds-and-thousands)

Right:
Frittelle di mele con gelato di vaniglia

CRESPELLE DI FRUTTA
Fruit crêpes

These little pancakes are best eaten as soon as they are ready.

Serves: 6; Preparation: 20 minutes + 2 hours for the fruit; Cooking: 15 minutes; Cooling: 15 minutes; Level of difficulty: Simple

Prepare the batter for the crêpes and chill in the refrigerator for 30 minutes. § Meanwhile, peel the fruit and slice thinly. Leave to macerate for 2 hours in the superfine sugar and lemon juice. § When the batter is ready, drain the fruit thoroughly. Add the vanilla extract and fruit to the batter. § Cook the crêpes in the usual way and serve hot, sprinkled with confectioners' sugar.

VARIATION
– Replace the apple, pear, and banana with fruits of the forest.

■ INGREDIENTS

- ½ quantity *Crêpes* (see recipe p. 14)
- 1 apple
- 1 pear
- 1 banana
- 1 tablespoon superfine (caster) sugar
- juice of 1 lemon
- 2–3 drops vanilla extract (essence)
- butter for frying
- confectioners' (icing) sugar for sprinkling

CRESPELLE CON PANNA E MARRONS GLACES
Crêpes with cream and marrons glacés

Serves: 8; Preparation: 20 minutes + 2 hours to rest; Cooking: 20 minutes; Level of difficulty: Medium

Mix both flours with the eggs, superfine sugar, and melted butter. Add the milk gradually, beating the mixture with a whisk to prevent lumps from forming. § Brush a nonstick skillet (frying-pan) with oil and heat to very hot. Pour in a small ladleful of batter, rotating the skillet so that the mixture spreads evenly. Cook the crêpe on both sides without browning. Continue this process until all the batter is used. § Whip the cream with the confectioners' sugar and mix the chopped marrons glacés in gently. § Fill the crêpes with this mixture and serve sprinkled with confectioners' sugar.

VARIATION
– Add a handful of chocolate chips and sprinkle with unsweetened cocoa powder.

■ INGREDIENTS

- 1 cup (3½ oz/100 g) chestnut flour, sifted
- 1 cup (3½ oz/100 g) all-purpose (plain) flour, sifted
- 3 eggs
- 1 tablespoon superfine (caster) sugar
- 3 tablespoons butter, melted
- 2 cups (16 fl oz/500 ml) milk
- ¾ cup (7 fl oz/200 ml) whipping (heavy) cream
- 2 tablespoons confectioners' (icing) sugar,
- 1 cup (8 oz/250 g) marrons glacés, chopped

Right:
Crespelle con panna e marrons glacés

INGREDIENTS

- 1 quantity *Crêpes*
  (see recipe p. 14)

- 1½ cups (12 oz/350 g)
  Mascarpone cheese
- 2 egg yolks
- ¾ cup (5 oz/150 g)
  superfine (caster) sugar
- 1 tablespoon rum
- grated zest of 1 lemon
- 2 tablespoons golden
  raisins (sultanas)
- butter for frying
- confectioners' (icing) sugar

CRESPELLE AL MASCARPONE
Crêpes with Mascarpone cheese

Serves: 8; Preparation: 20 minutes + 2 hours to rest; Cooking: 20 minutes; Level of difficulty: Medium

Prepare the crêpes. § Place the Mascarpone in a mixing bowl with the egg yolks, superfine sugar, rum, and lemon zest and beat until soft and creamy. Incorporate the golden raisins (sultanas). § Fill the crêpes with this mixture and serve hot, sprinkled with confectioners' sugar.

VARIATION
— Instead of golden raisins, use grated semi-sweet (dark) chocolate and sprinkle the crêpes with unsweetened cocoa powder.

CRESPELLE AI FICHI
Fig crêpes

■ INGREDIENTS

- 1 quantity *Crêpes* (see recipe p. 14)
- 10 figs (preferably black)
- 2 tablespoons grappa
- confectioners' (icing) sugar for sprinkling
- ⅓ cup (3½ fl oz/100 ml) heavy (double) cream

Serves: 8–10; Preparation: 20 minutes + 2 hours for the batter to rest; Cooking: 20 minutes; Level of difficulty: Medium

Prepare the crêpes. § Cut each fig into 4 segments. Place in a skillet (frying pan) and sprinkle with the grappa and a little confectioners' sugar. Cover and cook over low heat for 5–10 minutes. Leave to cool. § Whip the cream. § Fill the crêpes with the figs and serve sprinkled with confectioners' sugar. Serve the whipped cream separately.

VARIATIONS
– If fresh figs are not available, use fig jelly (jam).
– Add slivered (flaked) almonds to the filling.

BOMBOLONI
Italian doughnuts

■ INGREDIENTS

- 4 cups (1 lb/500 g) all-purpose (plain) flour,
- ⅔ cup (4 oz/125 g) superfine (caster) sugar
- dash of salt
- grated zest of 1 lemon
- 4 tablespoons butter, cut in small pieces
- 1 oz (30 g) fresh yeast or 2 (¼ oz/7.5 g) packages active dry yeast
- 4 tablespoons warm water
- oil for frying

An extremely popular recipe in Florence, these are a variation of the "krapfen" made in Alto Adige in the north. Children love them, and they are absolutely delicious served hot.

Makes: about 20 doughnuts; Preparation: 3½ hours; Cooking: 1 hour; Level of difficulty: Medium

Dissolve the yeast in a little warm water and set aside for 10 minutes. § Mix the flour (reserving 3 tablespoons) with one-third of the superfine sugar, the salt, and lemon zest. Make a well in the center and add the butter and then the yeast mixture. § Combine all the ingredients, and when the dough is soft and elastic, cover it and leave it to rest in a warm place for about 2 hours. § On a floured work surface roll the dough out to a thickness of ½ in (1 cm) and use a large upturned glass to cut out as many 3-in (8-cm) rings as possible. § Cover and leave to rise for another hour. § Heat the oil to very hot in a large skillet (frying pan) and fry a few at a time until golden brown. Drain on paper towels, then roll in the remaining superfine sugar and serve hot.

VARIATION
– Make a hole in the center of each doughnut and use a piping-bag to fill them with custard or jelly (jam).

Left:

Bomboloni

FRUIT AND ICE CREAM

Italian ice cream, called gelato, is famous throughout the world. It contains less sugar and fat then many other types, and generally has a much stronger flavor.

Fonduta al cioccolato
Chocolate fondue

This dessert is a delicious, eyecatching, and fun way to finish a dinner party!

Serves: 8; Preparation: 15 minutes; Cooking: 15 minutes; Level of difficulty: Medium

Wash the fruit and dry with care. Cut the larger pieces into bite-sized chunks. § If using apple, pear, or banana, immerse the chunks in water and lemon juice for a few seconds to prevent the flesh from browning, then dry carefully. § Arrange the fruit in an attractive bowl or serving dish. § Melt the chocolate in the top of a double-boiler over hot water. Dilute with the cream, then add the butter and superfine sugar and mix thoroughly. § Pour the chocolate mixture into a fondue bowl and keep warm over the flame. § Place bowls filled with the almonds, hazelnuts, and coconut on the table, so that diners can dip their pieces of fruit into them, after having dipped them in the chocolate sauce.

VARIATION
– Flavor the chocolate sauce with a small glass of rum.

■ INGREDIENTS

- about 2 lb (1 kg) mixed fresh fruit (strawberries, grapes, bananas, apples, apricots, peaches, figs, plums, pears, etc)
- 2 cups (16 fl oz/500 ml) water
- juice of 1 lemon
- 1 lb (500 g) semi-sweet (dark) chocolate, chopped
- 1 cup (7 fl oz/200 ml) light (single) cream
- 4 tablespoons butter
- 4 tablespoons superfine (caster) sugar
- ⅓ cup (1¾ oz/50 g) almonds, toasted and chopped
- ⅓ cup (1¾ oz/50 g) hazelnuts, toasted and chopped
- ½ cup (1¾ oz/50 g) shredded (desiccated) coconut

Fragole glassate
Glazed strawberries

Serves: 4-6; Preparation: 20 minutes + time to cool; Level of difficulty: Simple

Select the biggest and best strawberries. § Wash them in the white wine and dry carefully. § Melt the two chocolates in separate pans in the top of a double-boiler. Holding the strawberries by the stalks, dip some of them in the semi-sweet chocolate and some of them in the white chocolate. § Arrange on baking parchment (paper). Leave until the chocolate has solidified, then serve.

VARIATION
– Try dipping half of each strawberry first in the semi-sweet chocolate, then leave to dry before dipping the other half in the white chocolate. This way you will get two-tone strawberries.

■ INGREDIENTS

- 32 large strawberries, with stalks
- 1 cup (8 fl oz/250 ml) white dessert wine
- 3½ squares (3½ oz/100 g) semi-sweet (dark) chocolate
- 3½ squares (3½ oz/100 g) white chocolate

Right:
Fonduta al cioccolato

INGREDIENTS

- 6 large ripe yellow pears (Kaiser or Williams)
- 1⅓ cups (10½ oz/300 g) sugar
- dash of cinnamon
- 3½ squares (3½ oz/ 100 g) semi-sweet (dark) chocolate
- 1 quantity *Custard* using 3 eggs (see recipe p. 18)
- 6 Amaretti cookies (macaroons), store-bought (or see recipe p. 81), crumbled
- 4 tablespoons light (single) cream

PERE GLASSATE CON CREMA DI AMARETTI E CIOCCOLATO
Glazed pears with cream of macaroons and chocolate

Serves: 6; Preparation: 30 minutes; Cooking: about 1 hour; Level of difficulty: Complicated

Peel the pears, and without removing the cores, place them whole, in a high-sided, narrow saucepan. § Cover with cold water and stir in the sugar and cinnamon. Cook over low heat until tender but still firm, then remove from the saucepan and leave to cool. § Prepare the custard, stirring in the crumbled Amaretti cookies at the last minute. § Melt the chocolate in the top of a double-boiler. § Meanwhile, bring the cream to a boil, then use it to dilute the liquid chocolate. § Serve the pears in individual dishes, covered with the melted chocolate and on a bed of the custard-and-macaroon mixture.

VARIATION
— These chocolate-covered glazed pears are also delicious with vanilla or chocolate ice cream.

INGREDIENTS

- 2 cantaloupes (rock melons)
- 1 cup (8 oz/250 g) wild strawberries
- 24 strawberries
- 2 cups (16 fl oz/500 ml) white port
- 3 cups (24 fl oz/750 ml) sweet sparkling white wine
- juice of 1 lemon
- 4 tablespoons superfine (caster) sugar
- fresh mint leaves
- crushed ice

FRAGOLE E MELONE CON GHIACCIO ALLA MENTA
Strawberries and melon with mint-flavored ice

It is customary to eat melon with port and strawberries with champagne. I have combined the two with interesting results.

Serves: 6; Preparation: 20 minutes + time to chill; Level of difficulty: Simple

Use a melon-baller to carve the cantaloupes into balls, trying to waste as little as possible. § Place the melon balls in the bowl with the wild strawberries and the large strawberries sliced into segments. § Add the port, sparkling wine, lemon juice, superfine sugar, and mint leaves. Chill in the refrigerator for at least 1 hour. § Add the crushed ice just before serving.

VARIATION
— Prepare a mixture of raspberries, blackcurrants, and blueberries in the same way.

Left: *Pere glassate con crema di Amaretti e cioccolato*

TEGLIA DI PESCHE E FICHI
Peach and fig bake

Serves: 8; Preparation: 30 minutes; Cooking: about 40 minutes; Level of difficulty: Simple

Cut the figs and peaches into segments and arrange on a baking sheet lined with baking parchment (paper). § Sprinkle the peaches with a little of the superfine sugar and place the fruit under the broiler (grill) for about 10 minutes. § Meanwhile, whisk the egg yolks, the remaining superfine sugar, rusks, crumbled Amaretti cookies, and rum. Beat the egg whites with a dash of salt until stiff and fold them in. § Arrange the figs and peaches in a buttered ovenproof dish and pour the egg-and-rusk mixture over the top. Bake in a preheated oven at 350°F/180°C/gas 4 for about 30 minutes. § Serve the dessert while still warm.

VARIATION
– Serve with cream, lightly whipped with a dash of cinnamon.

■ INGREDIENTS

- 12 figs
- 6 peaches
- ½ cup (3½ oz/100 g) superfine (caster) sugar
- 6 egg yolks
- 10 rusks (Zwieback)
- 3 Amaretti cookies (macaroons), store-bought (or see recipe p. 81) and crumbled
- 4 tablespoons rum
- 3 egg whites
- dash of salt

PESCHE AL VINO CON ZABAIONE
Peaches and wine with zabaione

Peaches, wine, and cinnamon are a classic combination.
The addition of zabaione gives the dish an extra elegant touch.

Serves: 6; Preparation: 40 minutes; Cooking: 30 minutes; Level of difficulty: Medium

Place the wine, superfine sugar, cinnamon stick, and water in a large saucepan and bring to a boil. Boil for 5 minutes. § When the sugar has dissolved, immerse the peaches in this liquid and cook until tender but still firm. Remove from the saucepan and leave to cool. § Meanwhile, reduce the cooking juices over a high heat until they turn to syrup. § When this is cold, arrange it in individual dishes with the peaches and chill in the refrigerator. § Prepare the zabaione, then add to the peaches. Decorate each dish with ground pistachio nuts and serve.

VARIATION
– You will also get excellent results using pears instead of peaches.

■ INGREDIENTS

- 2 cups (16 fl oz/500 ml) strong white wine
- ½ cup (3½ oz/100 g) superfine (caster) sugar
- 1 stick cinnamon
- ½ cup (3½ oz/100 ml) cold water
- 6 peaches, peeled
- 1 quantity *Zabaione* (see recipe p. 20)
- 4 tablespoons pistachio nuts, ground

Right:
Pesche al vino con zabaione

ARANCE ALLO ZENZERO
Oranges with ginger

■ INGREDIENTS

• 6 oranges
• 4 tablespoons rum
• 4 tablespoons confectioners' (icing) sugar
• 4 tablespoons almonds, slivered (flaked)
• 1 teaspoon ginger, powdered

Serves: 6; Preparation: 20 minutes + time to cool; Level of difficulty: Simple

Peel the oranges, removing the white parts, then cut into small thin slices. Divide each slice in two. § Arrange the oranges in a serving dish with the rum, confectioners' sugar, almonds, and ginger. § Chill for a few hours, then serve.

VARIATION
– If you don't like ginger, flavor the oranges with a few drops of vanilla extract (essence).

PERE CON SALSA AI FRUTTI DI BOSCO
Pears with fruits of the forest sauce

■ INGREDIENTS

• 3 pears
• juice of 1½ lemons
• 1¾ cups (12 oz/350 g) superfine (caster) sugar
• 1 stick cinnamon
• 1¼ cups (10 oz/300 g) mixed fruits of the forest (raspberries, blackcurrants, blueberries, strawberries)
• 4 tablespoons water
• ½ cup (4 fl oz/125 ml) sweet dessert wine
• confectioners' (icing) sugar

Of all fruits, the pear is definitely the most suitable for cooking purposes. Adding different flavors enhances the flavor of the pear. The combination of pear and fruits of the forest works particularly well.

Serves: 6; Preparation: 20 minutes; Cooking: 20 minutes; Level of difficulty: Medium

Peel the pears and cut in half. Remove the cores and sprinkle with lemon juice to prevent the flesh from darkening. § Place in a small saucepan with enough water to just cover them, plus 1 cup (7 oz/200 g) of superfine sugar, the juice of half a lemon, and the cinnamon stick. Cook for about 15 minutes, or until they are tender but still firm. Remove from heat and leave to cool in their own syrup. § Meanwhile, take the fruits of the forest (reserving a few for decoration) and add the remaining superfine sugar, the water, the sweet white wine, and the juice of half a lemon. Place over low heat and cook until the mixture starts to thicken. § Purée the mixture in a food processor then push it through a fine-meshed strainer to remove the seeds. § Drain the pears, and place one pear half in each of six individual serving dishes. Cut into thin slices and place on top of a bed of fruits of the forest sauce. § Decorate with the reserved fruit, then sprinkle with confectioners' sugar, and serve.

Right:
Arance allo zenzero

Coppa al maraschino
Maraschino cup

Serves: 6; Preparation: 20 minutes + time to chill; Level of difficulty: Simple

Mix the Maraschino with the water and superfine sugar and leave for a few minutes to allow the sugar to dissolve. § Arrange the fruit in the bowl and pour the Maraschino mixture over it. Mix the ingredients together gently and chill for 1 hour before serving.

> VARIATION
> – Invent different combinations of fruit, choosing them on the basis of color.

■ INGREDIENTS

- 1 cup (8 fl oz/250 ml) Maraschino liqueur
- 1 cup (8 fl oz/250 ml) water
- 4 tablespoons superfine (caster) sugar
- 1¾ cups (14 oz/450 g) cherries
- 1¾ cups (14 oz/450 g) raspberries
- 1¾ cups (14 oz/450 g) wild strawberries

Composta di frutta estiva
Summer fruit compôte

Serves: 6; Preparation: 20 minutes; Cooking: 10 minutes; Level of difficulty: Simple

Dice the peaches and apricots. Halve the grapes, removing the seeds (pips). § Place the butter in a small saucepan and sauté the fruit. Add the superfine sugar and a dash of wine and cook for about 10 minutes. § When the compote is cold, mix in the strawberries. Serve decorated with lightly whipped cream and a sprinkling of chopped, toasted hazelnuts.

> VARIATION
> – Use other varieties of fruit too, provided the colors go together. For example, plums, cherries, and raspberries.

■ INGREDIENTS

- 8 oz (250 g) peaches
- 8 oz (250 g) apricots
- ⅓ cup (3½ oz/100 g) white grapes
- 3 tablespoons butter
- ½ cup (3½ oz/100 g) superfine (caster) sugar
- 1 cup (8 fl oz/250 ml) fruity white wine
- ¾ cup (3½ oz/100 g) strawberries
- ¾ cup (7 fl oz/200 ml) whipping cream
- hazelnuts, toasted and chopped, for sprinkling

Agrumi allo zucchero di canna
Citrus fruit with brown sugar

Serves: 6; Preparation: 20 minutes; Cooking: about 10 minutes; Level of difficulty: Simple

Slice the bananas and leave to soak for a few minutes in the lemon juice and an equal quantity of water. § Peel the grapefruit down to the flesh and slice with the oranges and tangerines. § Dry the bananas thoroughly and mix with the rest of the fruit. § Divide the fruit among individual serving dishes. Cover with plenty of brown sugar and place under a hot broiler (grill) until the sugar is caramelized. Serve at once.

> VARIATION
> – Pour a layer of *Vanilla pastry cream* (see recipe page 20) into the dish before adding the fruit.

■ INGREDIENTS

- 3 bananas
- juice of 1 lemon
- 3 pink grapefruit
- 3 oranges
- 3 tangerines
- brown sugar, to sprinkle over the fruit

Right:
Composta di frutta estiva

ALBICOCCHE AL CARTOCCIO
Apricot pockets

An effective way to savor all the fragrance of baked fruit.

Serves: 6; Preparation: 30 minutes; Cooking: 30 minutes; Level of difficulty: Simple

Place the wine, brown sugar, honey, and cinnamon in a saucepan and cook over a high heat until the mixture becomes syrupy. § Cut out 6 pieces of baking parchment (paper) with which to make pockets. § Place 2 pitted (stoned), halved apricots in each pocket. Pour a little of the syrup over them, then sprinkle with the crumbled Amaretti cookies and decorate with the pine nuts and raisins. Tie up the pockets with kitchen string and bake in a preheated oven at 400°F/200°C/gas 6 for about 15 minutes. § Serve while still warm.

VARIATION
— Peaches are also delicious prepared in this way.

■ INGREDIENTS

- 1 cup (8 fl oz/250 ml) white wine
- 4 tablespoons brown sugar
- 2 tablespoons honey
- ½ stick cinnamon
- 12 apricots
- 10 Amaretti cookies (macaroons), store-bought (or see recipe p. 81), crumbled
- 2 tablespoons pine nuts
- 2 tablespoons raisins

GRATIN DI PRUGNE
Plums au gratin

Serves: 6; Preparation: 30 minutes; Cooking: 10 minutes; Level of difficulty: Medium

Prepare the custard. § Cut the plums in half and pit (stone) them. § Combine the crumbled Amaretti cookies with the almonds and superfine sugar. § Place the plums in an ovenproof glass dish with the cut surfaces upward. Cover with the custard and sprinkle with the crumbled Amaretti mixture. § Place under a broiler (grill) and cook under high heat for about 10 minutes before serving.

VARIATION
— Replace the plums with the same quantity of peaches.

■ INGREDIENTS

- 1 quantity *Custard* (see recipe p. 18)
- 12 plums
- ⅔ cup (5 oz/150 g) Amaretti cookies (macaroons), store-bought (or see recipe p. 81), crumbled
- ⅔ cup (3 oz/90 g) almonds, slivered (flaked) and toasted
- 3 tablespoons superfine (caster) sugar

Right: *Albicocche al cartoccio*

- 8 peaches
- 3 tablespoons honey
- 1 cup (8 fl oz/250 ml) medium or sweet red wine

MACEDONIA DI PESCHE AL MIELE
Peaches with honey

Desserts made with wine, honey, and fruit date back to ancient Roman times.

Serves: 6; Preparation: 20 minutes; Chilling: 2-3 hours; Level of difficulty: Simple

Peel the peaches. Slice them thinly and place in a large serving bowl. § Dissolve the honey in the wine and pour over the peaches. Mix the peaches and wine together carefully. Chill in the refrigerator for at least 2–3 hours before serving.

VARIATION
– Add a dash of cinnamon to the wine and honey.

■ INGREDIENTS

- 3 medium-sized melons (Persian, Crenshaw, Cantaloupe, or Charentais)
- 2 cups (1 lb/500 g) mixed fruits of the forest (raspberries, blueberries, strawberries)
- juice of 1 lemon
- ½ cup (3½ oz/100 g) superfine (caster) sugar
- ⅔ cup (5 oz/150 g) raspberries
- ⅓ cup (3½ fl oz/100 ml) heavy (double) cream
- 2–3 drops vanilla extract (essence)

Meloncini al misto di bosco
Melons with fruits of the forest

Serves: 6; Preparation: 20 minutes; Level of difficulty: Simple

Cut the melons in half. Use a melon-baller to scoop out balls of melon and place them in a bowl. § Mix the melon balls carefully with the fruits of the forest, lemon juice, and half the sugar, then spoon them into the melon shells. § Beat the raspberries with the remaining sugar. Whip the cream with the vanilla extract. § Serve the fruit-filled melons with the whipped cream and raspberry sauce passed separately.

VARIATION
– Add a few tablespoonfuls of rum to the fruit.

■ INGREDIENTS

- 1 cup (7 oz/200 g) superfine (caster) sugar
- 2 cups (16 fl oz/500 ml) water
- juice of 4 lemons
- 2 egg whites
- dash of salt

DECORATION:

- 3 large peaches, peeled and thinly sliced
- 3 apricots, thinly sliced
- 2 tablespoons confectioners' sugar
- juice of 1 lemon

Sorbetto di limone con pesche e albicocche
Lemon sorbet with peaches and apricots

The word "sorbet" is probably of Arabic origin. It describes an extremely simple preparation based on a combination of sugar syrup and fruit juice, fruit purée, or liqueur.

Serves: 6; Preparation: 20 minutes + 3 hours to freeze; Cooking: 5 minutes; Level of difficulty: Simple

Prepare a syrup base by boiling the superfine sugar and water for a few minutes. Set aside until completely cool, then add the lemon juice. § Whisk the egg whites with a dash of salt until extremely stiff. Gradually stir in the lemon syrup, then place the mixture in the freezer. § Stir every 30 minutes to ensure that it freezes evenly, then whisk after 3 hours. Serve in individual dishes with the thinly sliced fruit sprinkled with confectioners' sugar and lemon juice.

Left:
Meloncini al misto di bosco

VARIATION
– The whisked egg whites are not essential – they simply make the sorbet creamier. You can make different flavored sorbets using the same process. All you have to do is add fruit pulp, wine, liqueurs, or other types of flavoring to the basic syrup.

Gelato alla crema con fragoline di bosco

Ice cream with wild strawberries

This is a basic recipe for ice cream. I am including simple instructions for making ice cream without an ice-cream machine. The results are a bit different from what we are used to, a little less delicate and more crystalline. But precisely for this reason, the recipe is somewhat special, and very good to eat. Prepare it a day in advance and whisk one last time before serving.

Serves: 4-6; Preparation: 30 minutes; Cooking: 15 minutes; Freezing: without an ice-cream machine, about 9 hours; Level of difficulty: Medium

Whisk the egg yolks and superfine sugar in a bowl until pale and creamy. § Bring the milk and cream to a boil, then set aside to cool for 10 minutes. Stir the milk and cream into the egg mixture. § Cook in the top of a double-boiler until the mixture is thick enough to coat the back of a spoon, making sure it never comes to a boil. Remove from heat and leave until completely cold. § Pour the cooled mixture into an ice-cream machine, if you have one, and follow the instructions to finish. § If you don't have an ice-cream machine, transfer the mixture to a large bowl and place in the freezer. After 3 hours, whisk the mixture to make sure it is freezing evenly. Return to the freezer for 3 hours, then whisk again. Whisk one last time after 3 more hours. § Place the wild strawberries in 4 to 6 individual ice cream dishes. Put scoops of ice cream on top and sprinkle with confectioners' sugar.

VARIATIONS
– Flavor the milk and cream with cinnamon or vanilla.
– Add ½ cup (3½ oz/100 g) crumbled Amaretti cookies (macaroons) to the beaten egg mixture to make Amaretti-flavored ice cream.

■ INGREDIENTS

BASIC MIXTURE:
- 4 egg yolks
- 1 cup (7 oz/200 g) superfine (caster) sugar
- 2 cups (16 fl oz/500 ml) milk
- 1 cup (8 fl oz/250 ml) light (single) cream

DECORATION:
- 2 cups (1 lb/500 g) strawberries
- confectioners' (icing) sugar for sprinkling

Gelato al cioccolato con lamponi e menta

Chocolate ice cream with raspberries and mint

Serves: 6; Preparation: 30 minutes; Cooking: 15 minutes; Freezing: without an ice-cream machine, about 9 hours; Level of difficulty: Medium

Prepare the ice cream according to the basic recipe above, dissolving the unsweetened cocoa in the hot milk and cream. § Place the raspberries in 6 individual ice cream dishes. Put scoops of ice cream on top and garnish with fresh mint.

VARIATION
– Top with whipped cream, or decorate with chocolate shavings.

■ INGREDIENTS

- 1 quantity ice cream mixture (see recipe above)
- 4 tablespoons unsweetened cocoa (cocoa powder)
- 2 cups (1 lb/500 g) raspberries
- fresh mint leaves for decoration

Right:
Gelato di crema con fragoline di bosco
and *Gelato di fragola*

INGREDIENTS

- 2 cups (16 fl oz/500 ml) milk
- 1 cup (8 fl oz/250 ml) light (single) cream
- 1 cup (7 oz/200 g) superfine (caster) sugar
- 1⅓ cups (10 oz/300 g) strawberries

GELATO ALLE FRAGOLE
Strawberry ice cream

Serves: 4-6; Preparation: 20 minutes; Cooking: 5 minutes; Level of difficulty: Simple

Boil the milk with the cream. Dissolve the superfine sugar in this mixture and leave to cool. § Purée the strawberries, then mix them with the milk and follow the recipe on page 118. § Serve in the individual ice-cream dishes.

VARIATIONS
– Serve with sliced strawberries sweetened with a little superfine sugar.
– Use different kinds of fruit to make ice cream – for example, peaches, apricots, berries, cherries, or bananas.

Index